ICONS
OF
GLORY

Prayers for Festivals and
Major Saints' Days

DAVID ADAM

kevin
mayhew

kevin
mayhew

First published in Great Britain in 2016 by Kevin Mayhew Ltd
Buxhall, Stowmarket, Suffolk IP14 3BW
Tel: +44 (0) 1449 737978 Fax: +44 (0) 1449 737834
E-mail: info@kevinmayhew.com

www.kevinmayhew.com

9 8 7 6 5 4 3 2 1 0

ISBN 978 1 84867 828 6
Catalogue No. 1501513

Cover design by Rob Mortonson
© Image used under licence from Shutterstock Inc.
Edited by Virginia Rounding
Typeset by Angela Selfe

Printed and bound in Great Britain

Contents

August

September

October

November

December

About the author

David Adam was the Vicar of Lindisfarne, off the Northumbrian coast, for thirteen years until he retired in March 2003. His work involved ministering to thousands of pilgrims and other visitors. He is the author of many inspiring books on spirituality and prayer, and his Celtic writings have rekindled a keen interest in our Christian heritage. For details of all David Adam's books published by Kevin Mayhew, please see our website: www.kevinmayhew.com

Introduction

While on the Holy Island of Lindisfarne, I was approached by a lady who told me how privileged I was. 'You are so fortunate to be surrounded by so many icons of glory. Not only Aidan, Cuthbert and the other saints, but the people who come as pilgrims, the birds, the flowers, the beauty: for all are icons of God.'

We appear too busy to allow glory to break into our lives. We are offered icon after icon of glory and yet we fail to see: it is as if our hearts are hardened and our eyes are blind. We do not create glory, it is all about us, and we need to open ourselves to it. God's world is full of his glory, he is ever present and within it (see Psalm 19:1-2). The world and all who live upon it are in the heart of God, and God is within the heart of every piece of his creation. If you have not experienced this, it is because you have not looked deep enough or long enough.

There is still more: 'God created humankind in his image, in the image of God he created them; male and female he created them' (Genesis 1:27). We are the icon of God. On the computer screen, an icon serves to lead us to what is behind the icon, to what it represents. You may like to keep this in mind when you consider how we learn to approach the mystery of God: it is through the mystery of ourselves. When we discover that our own being, in all its fullness, is simply beyond our human understanding, we can begin to find within us – and to see in others – the mystery of God. This should fill us with awe but not arrogance. As icons, we cannot treat each other with disrespect or neglect; rather, we should celebrate the special nature each of us has individually been given, our 'otherness', which reflects the great 'other' who is God. If you fail to be yourself, a light goes out on the earth, a light that only you can give. You can certainly learn from others and thereby gain insights and expand your talents, but God does not want you to be a copy of another person. We each of us experience life in our own way and have our own story to tell, our own song to sing and our own love to share. The icon explains nothing away: it points you to greater depths, into mysteries and reveals glory to you. Icons are able to tell you more than words can say. It is only when we realise we are a deep mystery and capable of revealing glory that we begin to discover our true nature.

Intercession is a good way to share with God all that is in your heart, knowing it is already in his heart, so your heart and his heart are one, you abide in him and he abides in you. Often, intercession is an opening of our heart to God and so getting a glimpse of glory. I believe that deep intercession begins in the heart. Go out from your prayers knowing that God is in your heart and in the hearts of all that you meet; return to your prayers with all that you have met and experienced in your heart to be joined to the heart of God. It is amazing how many situations are suddenly washed with a new brightness when we know that God is there and that God cares; intercession is a method of stopping and receiving icons of the hidden glory of God. Do remember that silence after any petition is important. Give people space to hold the prayer before God in love. Though I have offered a few ideas for each section, make them your own, and perhaps slim them down so that there is time for silence and being aware of God's love.

This book is to help you rise above the gloom and be open to the glory that is ever seeking to break through into your life. It is not a running away from reality but seeing that there is a greater depth to reality than we normally notice or feel. It is written for you to use at home or at church and so enrich your own prayers. The material for each saint's day or festival begins with a short introduction, and I would hope that you will find hints from the Bible readings to extend your own prayers.

The readings for each festival are from the Common Worship Lectionary as used by the Church of England, the Scottish Episcopal Church, the Church in Wales, and other churches within the Anglican Communion. This is very close to the Common Lectionary of the Roman Catholic Church, and is used by other denominations. I have written an opening prayer or 'collect' that is a prayer to help us collect and centre our thoughts, a list of intercessions, an offering of the peace and the blessing. All this could be used for a short service in a house group or in your home. Remember intercessions do not belong to the priests and minsters alone, but are very much your sharing in the prayers of the Church. The intercessions follow the pattern of many books of prayer: we pray in turn for the Church, the world, our homes and loved ones, for the sick and the needy, and finally we remember the saints and the departed. If you add the readings from the Lectionary to the prayers, spending some time in quiet and meditation, it will transform your worship at home, in church, and it will transform you also. Use this book as a means of opening up to the presence of God. May God help you to see you are yourself an icon of glory.

JANUARY

The Naming and Circumcision of Jesus

This festival is on the eighth day of the life of the child born of the Virgin Mary, and it is celebrated for three reasons. The first is the parents of Jesus fulfilling the covenant that God made with Abraham and having their child circumcised. The second is the naming of their child 'Jesus': the name means 'Yahweh saves'. The third is to note that this is the first shedding of the blood of Jesus.

Readings

Numbers 6:22-27
Psalm 8
Galatians 4:4-7
Luke 2:15-21

Opening prayer

Jesus, the only Son of the Father,
Our Lord and our God:
Jesus, we adore you.

Jesus, promised by the prophets,
Our Lord and our God:
Jesus, we adore you.

Jesus, proclaimed by the angels,
Our Lord and our God:
Jesus, we adore you.

Jesus, born of the Virgin Mary,
Our Lord and our God:
Jesus, we adore you.

Jesus, in your name we have life, and life eternal,
Our Lord and our God:
Jesus, we adore you.

Intercessions

Jesus, you are the Vine, we are the branches: may we know our common union with you, that you dwell in us and we dwell in you.

Jesus, empower us to go out in your name and bear fruit: may we tell of your presence and your love.

As you were poured out for others, may your Church give itself in the service of all.

We pray especially for your Church in [. . .]

Lord Jesus Christ, Son of God:

hear our prayer.

Jesus, Bread of Life, broken for us, we remember all who work for little reward.

We pray for all who are hungry and without food, resources or help.

We ask your blessing upon all who have been uprooted from their homes by war or disaster.

We remember those who are rich in material things but poor in spirit.

We come with our inner hunger to be filled, refreshed and restored.

Lord Jesus Christ, Son of God:

hear our prayer.

Jesus, the Gate and protector of your sheep, we ask your blessing upon our homes and families, upon our neighbours and our friends.

We pray for all who act as guardians or foster parents and for all children's homes.

We remember all who look after our communities and our cities.

We pray for all who risk their lives caring for others.

Lord Jesus Christ, Son of God:

hear our prayer.

Jesus, Good Shepherd, seeking out and caring for the lost, we pray for all who feel confused and lost.

We remember those who are without any helper and all whose lives are in danger.

Lord Jesus Christ, Son of God:

hear our prayer.

Jesus, Light of the World, shining in the darkness, we remember all whose lives are darkened by pain, sorrow or distress.
We pray for all who seek to bring comfort and relief to those who suffer.
We remember friends and loved ones who are ill, especially [. . .]
Lord Jesus Christ, Son of God:
hear our prayer.

Jesus, the Resurrection and the Life, in you are life, and life eternal.
You, Lord, are the hope of us all.
We remember before you our loved ones departed, and all your saints.
Merciful Father,
accept these prayers for the sake of your Son, our Saviour, Jesus Christ. Amen.

The peace

Jesus Christ is our Saviour; in his name are our hope and our peace.
The peace of the Lord be always with you.
And also with you.

Blessing

Go out in the mighty Name of the Father,
in the saving name of the Son,
in the powerful name of the Spirit:
and the blessing of God Almighty,
the Father, the Son and the Holy Spirit,
be upon you and remain with you always.
Amen.

The Conversion of St Paul

We celebrate the conversion of Saul, from being the persecutor of the Church to Paul the Apostle. This is related in the reading from Acts that is included in today's readings. There was the awareness of Jesus speaking to him, giving him the knowledge that to persecute the Church was to persecute its Lord. Paul would later tell of how we abide in the Lord and he in us. Then there was his temporary blindness and his healing. Though this was all of a sudden, his actual realisation of his call to proclaim Jesus to Jew and Gentile alike would take a while to develop. Yet he did act on the vision that he saw and so Saul became Paul.

Readings

Jeremiah 1:4-10
Psalm 67
Acts 9:1-22
Matthew 19:27-30

or

Acts 9:1-22
Psalm 67
Galatians 1:11-16a
Matthew 19:27-30

Opening prayer

Lord God, you call us into your light;
help us to be aware of you:
and to proclaim your love.

God, as we rejoice in your presence,
help us to be aware of you:
and to proclaim your love.

Open our eyes to behold you;
help us to be aware of you:
and to proclaim your love.

Open our ears to your call;
help us to be aware of you:
and to proclaim your love.

Open our whole being to your glory;
help us to be aware of you:
and to proclaim your love.

Intercessions

Lord our God, as we celebrate the life and witness of St Paul, we thank you for all who have helped us to know you, for all who have revealed your love and saving power to us.

We ask your blessing upon those who translate and provide the Scriptures, upon preachers and evangelists and all who witness to your love by their lives.

We remember all who are being persecuted or mocked and scorned for their faith.

We pray for those who are struggling with their faith at this time.

We ask your blessing upon all who support people in times of darkness and doubt.

Good and gracious God:
grant us a glimpse of your glory.

Lord our God, we remember all places where there is hatred and violence, where people's rights are denied and their freedom restricted; all who suffer under law where there is no love.

We pray for all freedom workers, all who work for liberty, compassion and peace.

We ask your blessing upon all who work in the transport of people or of produce.

We pray for all who travel by land, sea or air.

Good and gracious God:
grant us a glimpse of your glory.

Lord our God, we pray that our homes may reflect your love,
that our relationships may show your peace,
and that our lives may reveal your presence.
Lord, in all our dealings, free us from narrowness of vision.
Keep us from hardness of heart and give us compassion towards all.
Good and gracious God:
grant us a glimpse of your glory.

Lord our God, we remember all who suffer from blindness.
We pray for opticians, eye hospitals and the work of The Royal National
Institute of Blind People, and for Sightsavers.
We remember all who are disabled in any way, especially any who
live alone.
We pray for friends and loved ones who are ill at this time, especially
[. . .]
Good and gracious God:
grant us a glimpse of your glory.

Lord our God, make us aware of your saving power and grant us a
vision of life eternal.
We pray for all our loved ones departed, especially today for [. . .]
Merciful Father,
**accept these prayers for the sake of your Son, our Saviour, Jesus Christ.
Amen.**

The peace

The light of Christ shines in the darkness
and the darkness cannot overcome it.
The peace of the Lord be always with you.
And also with you.

Blessing

The God of grace open your eyes to his presence
that you may live to his glory:
and the blessing of God Almighty,
the Father, the Son and the Holy Spirit,
be upon you and remain with you always.
Amen.

FEBRUARY

Presentation in the Temple (Candlemas)

It is now 40 days since the birth of Jesus. Mary and Joseph took the child to the Temple in Jerusalem for the first time. As was required by Levitical law, Mary came to be 'cleansed' after the birth of a male child. Until that day Mary was not allowed to touch anything holy, or to enter a holy place. This is a common event in the Temple, yet it is transformed by two people. Simeon, a devout man, had a vision that he would not die until he had seen the Christ. He took Jesus in his arms and praised God that his eyes had seen God's salvation and declared Jesus as the 'Light to lighten the nations and for the glory of Israel'. The other person was Anna who was 84 years old. She also gave thanks, speaking about Jesus and redemption. It is the describing of Jesus as the Light that has made this day a celebration of Light conquering darkness.

Readings

Malachi 3:1-5
Psalm 24:1-6, 7-10
Hebrews 2:14-18
Luke 2:22-40

Opening prayer

Light of Christ:
shine upon us.

Lighten our eyes,
warm our hearts.
Light of Christ:
shine upon us.

Still our minds,
brighten our lives.
Light of Christ:
shine upon us.

Scatter the darkness
about us and within us.
Light of Christ:
shine upon us.

Intercessions

Lord God, as Jesus was brought into the Temple, may we know him in
this place.
Bless our churches with an awareness of his presence.
Give us grace to show the light of Christ in our lives and to see his
presence in each other.
We remember all who are being baptised or confirmed at this time,
and all lives which are dedicated to God.
As Joseph and Mary brought the infant Jesus to the Temple, we pray
that we may bring our young people to know and love you.
Jesus, light of the world:
fill our lives with your light.

As Simeon took Jesus in his arms and praised God, proclaiming Jesus
as the light to the nations:
we remember all who walk in darkness of war and violence,
all who suffer through the dark deeds of others.
We pray for all oppressed peoples, for the homeless, the refugees and
all unjustly imprisoned.
Jesus, light of the world:
fill our lives with your light.

As Anna awaited your coming and proclaimed you as the redeemer:
we pray for all who patiently wait for an awareness of you and your love.
We ask your light to shine in our homes and in all our dealings: that
your presence may be known to be among us.
We remember especially today all who feel rejected or unwanted.
Jesus, light of the world:
fill our lives with your light.

We remember before you, Lord, all whose lives are clouded with fear or anxiety, all who are worried or troubled or distressed.
We pray for all who suffer from depression and those tempted to end their lives.
We ask your blessing upon all who are ill at this time. We pray especially for […]
Jesus, light of the world,
fill our lives with your light.

We rejoice with all who have discovered the glorious liberty of the children of God.
We give thanks for the saints in light.
May our loved ones departed dwell in the fullness of light eternal.
We pray especially for […]
Merciful Father,
accept these prayers for the sake of your Son, our Saviour, Jesus Christ.
Amen.

The peace

Jesus is the Light of the World.
Let him fill your lives with his light and grant you peace.
The peace of the Lord be always with you.
And also with you.

Blessing

The light of Christ scatter the darkness from your hearts and minds;
the light of Christ shine in your hearts and homes;
the light of Christ guide you into the way of peace:
and the blessing of God Almighty,
the Father, the Son and the Holy Spirit,
be upon you and remain with you always.
Amen.

MARCH

St David

St David, the patron saint of Wales, was a monk and a bishop in the sixth century. It is almost certain that his main work was in the Pembrokeshire (Dyfed) area. The oldest writing about him comes from Ireland (c.730) and locates his monastery at Menevia, now St David's. His original monastery may have been at Henllan. David had the nickname Aquaticus, because those in his monasteries drank neither wine nor beer but only water, in the tradition of the monks of the Egyptian Desert. His name is often spelt as Dafydd, whence comes Taffy, a common name for a Welshman.

Readings

Ecclesiasticus 15:1-6 *or* Jeremiah 1:4-10
Psalm 16:2, 5-8
1 Thessalonians 2:2b-12
Matthew 16:24-27

Opening prayer

Good and gracious God, as we give thanks for St David, guide us:
and make us to be numbered with your saints.

Teach us to walk gently upon the earth:
and make us to be numbered with your saints.

Inspire us to be generous:
and make us to be numbered with your saints.

Help us to be more compassionate:
and make us to be numbered with your saints.

Empower us to reveal your love:
and make us to be numbered with your saints.

Intercessions

Father, we ask your blessing upon the Church in Wales.
We remember before you all churches dedicated to St David; we pray especially for St David's Cathedral.
We rejoice in the beauty and power of Welsh music, and pray for all who contribute to the Church in Wales through their hymns and their choirs.
We pray for those who translated the Scriptures and prayers into the Welsh language.
Grant your Church the vision to help to build up and to educate your people.
God, our hope and strength:
we put our trust in you.

Father, we pray for those who seek to maintain Welsh culture and traditions.
We ask your blessing upon the National Assembly for Wales and its contribution to the whole of Britain.
We pray for all who seek to walk gently upon the earth, caring for its resources and respecting all of God's creation.
Guide all who work in scientific research and who probe into the making of our world. May we all learn to love this world which you have made.
We remember all leaders of people, all teachers, all who influence the life of others.
God, our hope and strength:
we put our trust in you.

Father, we pray for all who build up community life and we pray for the communities to which we belong.
We ask your blessing upon our homes and all our relationships.
We pray for people who have newly moved into our community.
We ask your blessing upon all who are leaders and workers in our social lives.
God, our hope and strength:
we put our trust in you.

Father, we pray for all who are in trouble or difficulty at this time.
We pray for all who are unable to cope with life, due to poverty or illness.
We remember all who have been made homeless through violence or war.

We pray for all who are suffering in any way: we remember especially
[...]
God, our hope and strength:
we put our trust in you.

Father, we give thanks for St David and all the saints of Wales.
We pray for our loved ones departed, especially [...]
Lord, make them to be numbered with your saints, in glory everlasting.
Merciful Father,
**accept these prayers for the sake of your Son, our Saviour, Jesus Christ.
Amen.**

The peace

The God of hope fill you with all joy and peace in believing,
that you may abound in hope.
The peace of the Lord be always with you.
And also with you.

Blessing

May you see the presence of God in every face,
in every place,
in all of his creation:
and the blessing of God Almighty,
the Father, the Son and the Holy Spirit,
be upon you and remain with you always.
Amen.

St Patrick

St Patrick was born on the west coast of Britain about the year 390. He came from a Christian family. His father was a deacon and his grandfather a priest. At the age of 16, Patrick was captured by Irish raiders and taken to Ireland to be a slave. Here, possibly among other Christian captives, his faith grew strong. He says how he prayed a hundred times a day and as often at night. After six years of captivity he escaped on a ship. After some time he managed to return to his family. But he felt he was called to go back to Ireland and proclaim the Gospel. In the tradition of many Celtic saints he tended to walk rather than ride on his long journeys.

Readings

Tobit 13:1b-7 *or* Deuteronomy 32:1-9
Psalm 145:1-3
2 Corinthians 4:1-12
John 4:31-38

or

Isaiah 51:1-11
Psalm 96
Revelation 22:1-5
Matthew 10:16-23

Opening prayer

Lord, in your love,
we arise today.

In the presence of God our Creator,
in the peace of Christ our Saviour,
in the power of the Spirit our Helper:
Lord, in your love,
we arise today.

In the glory of the Father,
in the grace of the Son,
in the guiding of the Spirit:
Lord, in your love,
we arise today.

Intercessions

Father, as we give thanks for holy Patrick and his evangelising in Ireland, we pray for the Church in Ireland and for peace and unity.
We give thanks for all who have kept the faith in the difficult times.
We pray for all who witness that our God is not exclusive but is for all people, in all places and at all times.
We ask your blessing on all who make pilgrimages,
and for all churches dedicated to St Patrick.
Lord, raise us up:
to live in your presence.

Father, we ask your guidance
upon all who seek to bring liberty and freedom to our world;
upon all who seek to set free those held unjustly or who are treated as slaves.
We remember before you the work of Amnesty International.
Help us to see all refugees with compassion and understanding.
Lord, raise us up:
to live in your presence.

Father, we thank you for our homes, and loved ones;
may we show your peace, your love, your grace towards each other.
We ask your blessing upon people separated from loved ones.
We remember all who are lonely and in need of help.
Lord, raise us up:
to live in your presence.

Father, we remember before you all who are captive to addictions, to vice, to evil. May they discover the freedom that you offer them.
We remember all who are held by infirmity and illness, all who cannot cope on their own.

We bring before you all who have asked for our prayers; [. . .]
Lord, raise us up:
to live in your presence.

Father, we give thanks that St Patrick witnessed to the resurrection:
may we know the power of Christ's resurrection in our lives today.
We remember our loved ones departed, whom we hold still in our
hearts, praying especially for [. . .]
Lord, raise us up:
to live in your presence.

Merciful Father,
accept these prayers for the sake of your Son, our Saviour, Jesus Christ.
Amen.

The peace

In Christ is the presence of God,
the power of God
and the peace of God.
The peace of the Lord be always with you.
And also with you.

Blessing

The goodness of God guide you.
The grace of God go with you.
The hand of God protect you:
and the blessing of God Almighty,
the Father, the Son and the Holy Spirit,
be upon you and remain with you always.
Amen.

St Joseph

St Joseph was engaged to Mary when he was told she was with child from the Holy Spirit. He was thinking of dismissing her when the angel of the Lord appeared to him in a dream. The angel told him to take Mary as his wife and to name the child Jesus, 'for he will save his people from their sins' (Matthew 1:18-25). Then after the birth of Jesus in Bethlehem, Joseph had another dream and the angel directed him to escape with the child and his mother to Egypt (Matthew 2:13-15). When Herod died, Joseph had a third dream in which the angel told him to return to Israel. Joseph decided Judea was too dangerous for the child, so he took him to live in Nazareth in the district of Galilee. When Jesus was 12, his parents took him up to the Temple in Jerusalem for the Passover festival. Jesus stayed on in the Temple and, after having found him again, Mary said, 'Look, your father and I have been searching for you in great anxiety' (Luke 2:41-51). Here, Joseph and Mary are described as the 'parents' and Joseph as the 'father' of Jesus. In his home town the people said of him, 'Is not this the carpenter's son? Is not his mother called Mary?' (Matthew 13:55). Again there is the acknowledgement of Joseph being seen as his father. It is through Joseph that Jesus is 'of the house of David'.

Readings

2 Samuel 7:4-16
Psalm 89:26-36
Romans 4:13-18
Matthew 1:18-25

Opening prayer

Jesus, born of the Blessed Virgin Mary:
come, lighten our darkness.

Jesus, cared for by Joseph:
come, lighten our darkness.

Jesus, growing up in a family unit:
come, lighten our darkness.

Jesus, revealed in glory:
come, lighten our darkness.

Jesus, here and with us now:
come, lighten our darkness.

Intercessions

Lord God, we give thanks this day for St Joseph.
We ask your blessing upon all churches and communities dedicated in his name.
We remember all who are guardians of the faith, all who preach the word of God.
We pray for all theological colleges and for those who are preparing for ordination.
We remember all who are struggling with their faith and those beset by doubt.
Lord, we trust in you:
hear us and help us.

Lord God, we give thanks for Joseph's care and love of Jesus.
We pray for all who are carers, guardians and protectors.
We ask your blessing upon all who foster children and on those who adopt them.
We pray for all care homes and especially for [. . .]
We give thanks for Joseph, the carpenter.
We remember all carpenters, joiners and workers in wood.
We pray for all craftspeople, musicians and artists.
Lord, we trust in you:
hear us and help us.

Lord God, we give thanks that Jesus was brought up within a loving family.
Help us to know your presence in our homes, and see your presence in each other.

We pray for homes where there is little love, where relationships are
breaking down,
and for children who are taken into care.
Lord, we trust in you:
hear us and help us.

Lord God, as we give thanks for the protection of Joseph:
we remember all who need protection and care.
We ask your blessing on children who are misused or abused.
We pray for all who have no helper, for refugees and homeless people.
We remember the ill and the frail and all who are in hospital.
We remember loved ones who are ill and pray especially for [...]
Lord, we trust in you:
hear us and help us.

Lord God, with you as our protector and guardian, we ask you to keep
us in life eternal.
We pray for our loved ones departed, especially for [...]:
that they may rejoice in the fullness of eternal life.
Merciful Father,
accept these prayers for the sake of your Son, our Saviour, Jesus Christ.
Amen.

The peace

Do not be afraid: the Lord is with you.
He will keep you in peace.
Trust in the Lord with all your heart.
The peace of the Lord be always with you.
And also with you.

Blessing

The goodness of God, the love of Christ
and the power of the Holy Spirit
guard you and keep you from all evil:
and the blessing of God Almighty,
the Father, the Son and the Holy Spirit,
be upon you and remain with you always.
Amen.

The Annunciation of Our Lord to the Blessed Virgin Mary

Today marks an event that transforms our understanding of God. In his love he seeks to send his Son into the world. Jesus is to share in our humanity that we may share in his divinity. God seeks permission of Mary, for God does not force his will upon us. He sends his messenger, the angel Gabriel, to tell Mary of the birth: and Mary assents in the words 'let it be with me according to your word' (Luke 1:38). The Christian Church has celebrated this festival since the fourth century. This festival is centred on Mary and her willingness to serve God: in England it became known as 'Lady Day'.

Readings

Isaiah 7:10-14
Psalm 40:5-11
Hebrews 10:4-10
Luke 1:26-38

Opening prayer

Lord God, in Jesus you shared in our humanity.
May we abide in you:
and know you abide in us.

You came down to raise us up.
May we abide in you:
and know you abide in us.

You became human that we might share in the divine.
May we abide in you:
and know you abide in us.

Intercessions

Father, you chose the Virgin Mary to be the mother of your Son.
We ask your blessing upon those who quietly serve you in their daily lives and work.
We remember all who dedicate their lives to you.
Lord, strengthen all who face mocking or scorn because of their faith.
We pray for all whose faith is weak and who are afraid to witness to your love.
Let the Church without fear reach out to all nations and peoples.
Father, through your angel, Gabriel, you reminded Mary that you are with her, in the words, 'The Lord is with you'. May we know he is with us too, and with all people.
Lord, ever with us, we trust in you:
hear our prayer.

Father, in Christ's coming you offered peace on earth to us all.
We ask your blessing upon the nations of the world, that in you they may find peace.
We pray for all who seek to bring peace and goodwill to our world.
We pray for the work of the United Nations and all peace-keeping forces.
We remember especially [. . .]
Lord, ever with us, we trust in you:
hear our prayer.

Father, by the willingness of Mary and the power of the Holy Spirit, your Son came to dwell among us.
Open our homes, our hearts and our lives to receive Christ.
We pray for each home in our community.
We pray for all religious communities, especially those dedicated to St Mary.
Lord, ever with us, we trust in you:
hear our prayer.

Father, by Mary and Joseph, Jesus was cared for and protected.
In compassion may we care for the hungry and those without any helpers.
We remember all who are ill or in need.
We remember especially [. . .]
Lord, ever with us, we trust in you:
hear our prayer.

As promised, our Lord came down that he may raise us up:
he came as our Saviour, he died that we might live.
We remember our loved ones departed, and pray today especially for
[…]
Merciful Father,
accept these prayers for the sake of your Son, our Saviour, Jesus Christ.
Amen.

The peace

The peace of God the Creator,
the peace of Christ the Redeemer,
the peace of the Holy Spirit:
the peace of the Holy three
be about you and within you.
The peace of the Lord be always with you.
And also with you.

Blessing

In the tender compassion of our God,
the Light of Christ dwell among you,
shine upon you,
and guide your feet into the way of peace:
and the blessing of God Almighty,
the Father, the Son and the Holy Spirit,
be upon you and remain with you always.
Amen.

APRIL

St George

St George died as a Christian martyr about the year 304 at the beginning of the Diocletian persecution. He was most likely a soldier in Palestine, dying at Lydda, where his tomb was to be seen. He was given the title 'Great Martyr' in the eastern Mediterranean. There were Christian churches dedicated to St George in England before the Norman Conquest. He was known as a martyr when Bede was writing in the seventh and eighth centuries. St George was adopted as the patron saint of soldiers. During the Crusades, returning soldiers brought back the cult of St George as their patron. Richard I placed himself under the patronage of St George. It was after Agincourt that Henry V declared George as the patron of England. Edward III founded under his patronage the Order of the Garter, for which was built St George's Windsor under Edward IV and Henry VII.

Readings

1 Maccabees 2:59-64 *or* Revelation 12:7-12
Psalm 126
2 Timothy 2:3-13
John 15:18-21

Opening prayer

From the hatred that divides people from people:
Good Lord, deliver us.

From the greed that exploits the earth:
Good Lord, deliver us.

From our indifference towards the oppressed:
Good Lord, deliver us.

From all that ignores the dignity of others:
Good Lord, deliver us.

From all that diminishes beauty and love:
Good Lord, deliver us.

From our unwillingness to stand up for justice:
Good Lord, deliver us.

Intercessions

Father, we give thanks for St George and all who have died for their faith.
We pray for all communities and churches dedicated in the name of
St George.
We remember before you all Christians who are being persecuted at
this time.
We give thanks for all who have shared their faith with us,
for the writers and preachers, for hymn writers and musicians.
May we learn to share our faith and bring others to know you and
your love.
Lord, hear us:
and help us.

Father, as we remember St George,
we ask your blessing upon all who strive for freedom and truth,
all who stand up for the poor and oppressed,
all who seek peace and unity in areas of conflict,
and all who seek to restore broken relationships.
Lord, hear us:
and help us.

Today we ask your blessing upon England,
upon the royal family and all leaders in Parliament.
We give you praise for the freedom we have.
Lord, bless our homes with your peace, our lives with your love.
Lord, hear us:
and help us.

Father, we praise you for our salvation in Christ Jesus.
We pray for all who battle against their own demons and dragons.
We remember those who are addicted, or held captive by vice.

We pray for all who are struggling with illness, especially for [...]
Lord, hear us:
and help us.

Father, we give thanks that, in you and your love, victory is ours, and
life is stronger than death.
We give thanks for St George and all your saints.
We pray for all who are departed from us, especially [...]:
may they enjoy the peace of your eternal presence.
Merciful Father,
accept these prayers for the sake of your Son, our Saviour, Jesus Christ.
Amen.

The peace

Do not walk in darkness, but in the light and love of the Lord.
The peace of the Lord be always with you.
And also with you.

Blessing

Know that God is your strength and salvation,
he is your light and your life:
and the blessing of God Almighty,
the Father, the Son and the Holy Spirit,
be upon you and remain with you always.
Amen.

St Mark the Evangelist

St Mark is thought to be the earliest writer of a Gospel. According to the Acts of the Apostles he was the son of Mary who lived in Jerusalem. It was to their house that Peter went when he escaped from prison. According to Paul, Mark was a cousin of Barnabas (Colossians 4:10). Mark accompanied Paul and Barnabas on their first missionary journey but for some reason left them at Perga to return to Jerusalem (Acts 13:13). Later he accompanied Barnabas to Cyprus (Acts 13, 15). He was with Paul when he was under house arrest in Rome (Colossians 4:10). In the letter to Philemon, (verse 24), Paul numbers Mark among his fellow workers. Again writing to Timothy, he asks for Mark to be brought to him for he is 'a most useful servant to me' (2 Timothy 4:11). Peter also mentions he was with him in Rome and affectionately calls him his 'son' (1 Peter 5:13). The Gospel bearing Mark's name was most likely written in Rome and was based on the teaching and preaching of St Peter and on Mark's own memory. Because Mark has this close link with Peter there is a feeling of immediacy in the Gospel bearing his name. The symbol for St Mark in art is a lion, for Mark depicts the kingship and strength of Jesus who is ever watchful.

Readings

Proverbs 15:28-33 *or* Acts 15:35-41
Psalm 119:9-16
Ephesians 4:7-16
Mark 13:5-13

Opening prayer

Lord, open our eyes to your presence:
in the world and in each other.

Lord, open our ears to your call:
in the poor and in the needy.

Lord, open our hearts to your love:
revealed in our loved ones and friends.

Lord, open our lives to your glory:
that we may know we dwell in you, and you in us.

Intercessions

Holy God, Holy and Strong One, we give you thanks for St Mark: for his friendship with Saints Barnabas, Paul and Peter; for his missionary journeys and for the Gospel that bears his name.
We pray for all peoples and places dedicated in the name of St Mark: we remember Venice and St Mark's Basilica.
We ask your blessing upon all who seek to share their faith, and all who inspire others by their lives and their love.
We pray for the outreach of the Church and for guidance in our own witness to your love.
We remember the Bible Society, the Scripture Union, and all who seek to make available the word of God through publishing.
Loving God, we come to you:
hear us and help us.

Holy God, Holy and Strong One, we remember before you all who seek to protect the vulnerable and the threatened in our world:
not only the humans but also the wild life and the great rainforests.
We ask your blessing upon all who risk their lives in the care of others and in the protection of the world and its resources.
We pray for scientists, those working in conservation, all who provide us with food through their labours.
Loving God, we come to you:
hear us and help us.

Holy God, Holy and Strong One, we give you thanks for those who have cared for us, loved us and shared their lives with us.
We ask your blessing upon our families and friends.
We pray for those caring for loved ones and neighbours in their need, and for all the systems that support them.
We pray for home help services, the social services and all care homes.

Loving God, we come to you:
hear us and help us.

Holy God, Holy and Strong One, we come to you in weakness for new strength.
We come to you in trouble for your peace.
We come to you in darkness for your light.
We come to you in illness for your healing.
We remember all who are suffering in our world, especially those who have no one to care for them.
We pray for friends and loved ones who are ill, especially [. . .]
Loving God, we come to you:
hear us and help us.

Holy God, Holy and Strong One, you are the Lord of the living and the dead.
We give thanks for the life of St Mark, and for our loved ones in glory.
We pray especially today for [. . .]
Merciful Father,
**accept these prayers for the sake of your Son, our Saviour, Jesus Christ.
Amen.**

The peace

Let the Word of God be a lantern to your feet and a light to your path, to bring you into the way of peace.
The peace of the Lord be always with you.
And also with you.

Blessing

With your whole heart, seek the Lord.
With your lips, tell of his goodness.
With your mind, meditate upon him.
With all your attention, give yourself to him:
and the blessing of God Almighty,
the Father, the Son and the Holy Spirit,
be upon you and remain with you always.
Amen.

MAY

1 MAY

St Philip and St James

Philip and James were part of the original twelve disciples. Philip came from Bethsaida in Galilee. He was called by Jesus and as a result brought Nathaniel to follow Jesus. When the Greeks wanted to meet Jesus, they first approached him through Philip. In early manuscripts 1 May was his feast day. James is known as 'the Less' to distinguish him from James the brother of John and son of Zebedee. This James is the son of Alphaeus; he may also be James the Younger, who in Mark's Gospel is a witness to the crucifixion. Both saints are commemorated on this day because the church in Rome where their relics rest was dedicated on this day in the year 560.

Readings

Isaiah 30:15-21
Psalm 119:1-8
Ephesians 1:3-10
John 14:1-14

Opening prayer

In this church where we worship:
open our hearts to your presence.

In our home and with our family:
open our hearts to your presence.

In our work and in our leisure:
open our hearts to your presence.

In every meeting with another person:
open our hearts to your presence.

Intercessions

Father, we give you thanks and praise for the lives and witness of the apostles St Philip and St James.
We remember all those whose work and lives reveal your love and your salvation.
Help us also, Lord, to trust in you and to live to your glory.
May we show you are our God by the way we live our lives.
Lord, give us the strength to share in your saving work.
We ask your blessing upon the Church working among the outcasts and oppressed, and on those who are seeking to reach the hard-hearted and the cynical.
God, in your gracious love:
Hear us and bless us.

Father, we remember before you nations making decisions that affect the world's environment.
Lord, by your Holy Spirit, guide all leaders and heads of state:
give them wisdom and courage in their decisions.
Bless all who are seeking to bring peace and well-being to our world.
We pray for those who seek to protect endangered species and the rainforests.
God, in your gracious love:
Hear us and bless us.

Father, we give thanks for all who have enriched our lives by their love.
We remember our parents, teachers and all who have cared for us.
Bless our homes with your peace and fill them with your light and love.
We pray for the communities to which we belong and the places where we work.
God, in your gracious love:
Hear us and bless us.

Father, you seek and save the lost.
We remember before you all who have lost their way:
those who are strangers to the truth,
those who are not living life in its fullness.
We pray for those being led astray by others,

and for all who are misled by the world and wrong advice.
We bring before you friends and loved ones who are ill:
we pray especially for [...]
God, in your gracious love:
Hear us and bless us.

Father, you created us out of love and for your love.
We commit our loved ones departed to your love and to life eternal.
Merciful Father,
**accept these prayers for the sake of your Son, our Saviour, Jesus Christ.
Amen.**

The peace

The Lord God waits to be gracious to you.
In returning to him and rest, you shall be saved.
In quietness and trust, let the Lord be your strength.
The peace of the Lord be always with you.
And also with you.

Blessing

Do not let your hearts be troubled.
Trust in God, in Christ, the Prince of Peace,
and in the power of the Holy Spirit:
and the blessing of God Almighty,
the Father, the Son and the Holy Spirit,
be upon you and remain with you always.
Amen.

St Matthias

After the death of Judas, the disciples put forward two possible people, Joseph Barsabbas and Matthias to bring their number back up to twelve. Matthias was then chosen by lot to show the choice was not theirs but God's. However, qualifications for a chosen person were declared by the disciples: the person chosen had to have been with Jesus during his ministry and to have been witness to his resurrection. (Acts 1:15-26). Matthias was present with the other eleven when they received the Holy Spirit at Pentecost. Little else is known for sure about Matthias.

Readings

Isaiah 22:15-25
Psalm 15
Acts 1:15-26
John 15:9-17

or

Acts 1:15-26
Psalm 15
1 Corinthians 4:1-7
John 15:9-17

Opening prayer

Lord, through your love for us, may we know you
and the power of your resurrection.

Lord, in our prayers and in stillness, may we know you
and the power of your resurrection.

Lord, in light and in darkness, may we know you
and the power of your resurrection.

Lord, in life and in death, may we know you
and the power of your resurrection.

Intercessions

Loving Father, we praise you and give thanks for the life and witness of St Matthias.
We give thanks for all those throughout the ages who have witnessed to you and to the power of the resurrection of our Lord.
Strengthen your Church that it may witness to your love and to your abiding presence.
We remember those who quietly witness to you by their lives and their attitude to creation.
We ask your blessing upon all who are staying firm in their faith when they are being punished for it.
Lord, give us the courage to witness to you and the power of the resurrection.
Lord, you know everyone's heart:
hear us and help us.

Loving Father, we remember before you all who are seeking work, who are facing interviews or election to office.
We ask your blessing on all who are unemployed, or used as cheap labour, and those who are given a poor price for their goods.
We pray that justice and fair dealing may prevail in our world: that all people will be treated with respect and care.
We pray for all support agencies and for those who give help and guidance to those in need.
Lord, you know everyone's heart:
hear us and help us.

Loving Father, we give you thanks for friends who have shared their lives and faith with us.
We remember before you all who have guided and inspired us.
May we be good friends to those we are able to share with.
We pray for people who have moved into the area where we live; may they find us welcoming and helpful.
Lord, you know everyone's heart:
hear us and help us.

Loving Father, we give you thanks and praise for our lives and the opportunity to know and love you.

We bring before you the troubles and sorrows of our world; we pray for all who are suffering through acts of terrorism or violence.
We remember all who are impoverished through the greed of others.
We pray for all who are ill, and for those awaiting medical treatment; we pray especially for [. . .]
Lord, you know everyone's heart:
hear us and help us.

Loving Father, we rejoice that our Lord is risen and in him is life eternal.
We pray for friends and loved ones departed from us; especially today we remember [. . .]
Merciful Father,
**accept these prayers for the sake of your Son, our Saviour, Jesus Christ.
Amen.**

The peace

Abide in God's love and in the love of Christ, his Son, our Lord.
The peace of the Lord be always with you.
And also with you.

Blessing

Learn to walk in the way of his saints,
in faith, hope and love:
and the blessing of God Almighty,
the Father, the Son and the Holy Spirit,
be upon you and remain with you always.
Amen.

The Visit of the Blessed Virgin Mary to Elizabeth

Today's Gospel describes the visitation of Mary to her cousin Elizabeth. The first recorded celebration of this as a festival day was in 1263 at a Franciscan Order General Chapter, but it soon spread throughout Europe. Because it is an event mentioned in the Gospel, the churches at the Reformation did not remove it as they did some of the other Marian festivals, especially as it was the occasion when Mary praised her Lord in the words of the Magnificat. Luke would have us believe that the leaping of the baby in the womb was the reaction of John the Baptist to Jesus, even before either was born.

Readings

Zephaniah 3:14-18
Psalm 113
Romans 12:9-16
Luke 1:39-49, 50-56

Opening prayer

Dearest Lord, let our love be genuine.
Lord, renew us in your love.

May we hate all that is evil.
Lord, renew us in your love.

Help us to hold fast to what is good.
Lord, renew us in your love.

Teach us to honour one another.
Lord, renew us in your love.

May we serve you faithfully in love.
Lord, renew us in your love.

Intercessions

Loving Lord, we give thanks for the visitation of Mary to Elizabeth and the support they gave each other.

We pray for all who are pregnant, and for all who support them: we pray for maternity units and for nursing care.

We rejoice that you have called us to know you and to love you: that you have done great things for us. Let us not take for granted all that you have provided for us.

We pray that your Church may help to show your salvation to the world; may it reveal your love and your peace.

We call upon you, Lord:

give strength to your people.

Loving Lord, we ask your blessing upon all who work among the poor and lowly:

on those who seek to raise standards, to bring about fair trade, and to relieve poverty.

We pray for all governments and research workers in seeking to feed the hungry.

We give thanks and pray for the farming communities of our world and all who provide us with our produce and needs.

We call upon you, Lord:

give strength to your people.

Loving Lord, we give thanks for our parents and our families, especially those who have cared for us and protected us.

We pray for children who feel unloved or unwanted, for all who are neglected or abused.

We ask your blessing upon all who are in need of friendship or help. Lord, bless our homes, our loved ones and our friends.

We call upon you, Lord:

give strength to your people.

Loving Lord, we give thanks for all who share in your healing, and bring peace and justice to peoples and nations.

We remember all who are struggling with ill health or who are terminally ill.

We pray for the work of the hospice movement.

We remember especially today [...]
We call upon you, Lord:
give strength to your people.

Loving Lord, we thank you for your power to renew and restore us.
We pray for all who are bereaved at this time, for those feeling lost
and alone.
We ask your blessing upon all the departed that, through your grace,
they may rejoice in glory.
We pray especially for [...]
Merciful Father,
**accept these prayers for the sake of your Son, our Saviour, Jesus Christ.
Amen.**

The peace

The Lord is in your midst;
he will rejoice over you with gladness;
he will renew you in his love and peace.
The peace of the Lord be always with you.
And also with you.

Blessing

God's eye be on you,
God's hand uphold you,
God's love enfold you,
God's power renew you:
and the blessing of God Almighty,
the Father, the Son and the Holy Spirit,
be upon you and remain with you always.
Amen.

JUNE

St Barnabas

Barnabas, meaning 'Son of Consolation', was a Levite from Cyprus. Like Paul he was from the Greek-speaking world. He is first heard of when selling his estate and giving the proceeds to the early Church, where all was held in common. He was not one of the original apostles, according to the Evangelists. Yet he was soon numbered among the apostles and is one of their most noted members in Acts. He introduced Paul to the Church in Jerusalem. At the Council in Jerusalem, Barnabas spoke up for Gentile Christians. According to Paul, Barnabas was a cousin of Mark (Colossians 4:10), the writer of St Mark's Gospel. Mark accompanied Paul and Barnabas on their first missionary journey, but left them at Perga to return to Jerusalem (Acts 13:13). Mark later accompanied Barnabas to Cyprus (Acts 13, 15).Tradition has it that Barnabas was martyred in Cyprus in the year 61.

Readings

Job 29:11-16
Psalm 112
Acts 11:19-30
John 15:12-17

or

Acts 11:19-30
Psalm 112
Galatians 2:1-10
John 15:12-17

Opening prayer

Lord, in the joys of living
be with us:
enfold us in your love.

Lord, in our family lives
be with us:
enfold us in your love.

Lord, in our hopes and fears
be with us:
enfold us in your love.

Lord, in our success and failures
be with us:
enfold us in your love.

Lord, in our reaching out and caring
be with us:
enfold us in your love.

Intercessions

Loving God, we rejoice in your love and care.
We give you thanks for the compassion and generosity of Barnabas
and for his bringing of St Paul to the Church in Jerusalem.
Help us to be compassionate in our dealings and generous in our
attitude towards others. May your Church be welcoming to all who
turn to her.
May we deal gently and with love towards those who are new to the
faith and those who are struggling with their faith.
We pray for the outreach of our church and its ability to proclaim
Christ as Lord.
God, as you love us all:
teach us to love one another.

Loving God, we remember people on the fringes of society and those
who feel badly treated.
We pray for all who feel isolated by poverty, or because of their colour
or religion.
We remember those forced to live in ghettoes and in shanty towns, and
those who live on the streets of our cities.

We ask your blessing upon all agencies that reach out to help those who are in need: we pray especially for [. . .]
God, as you love us all:
teach us to love one another.

Loving God, we give thanks for all who have revealed your love to us by their generosity in the giving of their time and their attention.
For those who have helped us to grow and those who have shared in our education.
We ask your blessing upon our homes and the homes of our community: may they be places of love and acceptance.
We pray for any homes where members feel discouraged or unwanted, or who are treated meanly. Lord, may we deal with all people with dignity and respect.
God, as you love us all:
teach us to love one another.

Loving God, we give you praise for our lives on this earth and for our abilities.
We remember all who are not easily accepted in society through disfigurements, dementia or mental illness.
We pray for those who are prejudiced against others because of their race or position in society.
We ask your blessing upon all who care for the ill, whoever they are.
We remember friends and loved ones who are suffering at this time, especially [. . .]
God, as you love us all:
teach us to love one another.

Loving God, we rejoice in the saints of your Church and who are in life eternal.
We give thanks today especially for St Barnabas, St Paul and St Mark.
We pray for all who have died today and all who are bereaved.
We remember our loved ones departed. We pray especially for [. . .]
Merciful Father,
accept these prayers for the sake of your Son, our Saviour, Jesus Christ. Amen.

The peace

Love one another as God loves you. As God holds you in his heart, hold each other in your hearts.
The peace of the Lord be always with you.
And also with you.

Blessing

Love the Lord your God and his creation
with all your heart, mind, soul, and strength:
and the blessing of God Almighty,
the Father, the Son and the Holy Spirit,
be upon you and remain with you always.
Amen.

The Birth of John the Baptist

John was the son of Zechariah, a Temple priest, and Elizabeth who was cousin to the Virgin Mary. He was born when his mother was advanced in years, after the foretelling by an angel. The first meeting of John and Jesus was when they were both still in the womb, and it was said John leaped for joy at the coming of the Lord. Then, we hear no more of John until he starts baptising in the Jordan and preaching about the year 27. In appearance and life style, he resembled an Old Testament prophet. His message was one of repentance and preparation for the Messiah. When he baptised Jesus, he recognised him as the Messiah. After denouncing the incestuous marriage of Herod Antipas, John was imprisoned and finally put to death. As the Gospel has his birthday six months before Jesus, his birthday is held on 24 June and that of Jesus on 25 December. John's feast is at the end of the summer solstice as the days begin to shorten. Jesus is after the winter solstice as the days begin to lengthen. So in a sense this mirrors John's words: 'He must increase, but I must decrease' (John 3:30).

Readings

Isaiah 40:1-11
Psalm 85:7-13
Acts 13:14b-26 *or* Galatians 3:23-29
Luke 1:57-66, 80

Opening prayer

Lord, you are here,
in your grace and goodness:
grant us your peace.

Here in your light and your love,
in your grace and goodness:
grant us your peace.

Here in your power and your peace,
in your grace and goodness:
grant us your peace.

Here in your greatness and gentleness,
in your grace and goodness:
grant us your peace.

Here in your strength and salvation,
in your grace and goodness:
grant us your peace.

Intercessions

God, our Father, as we give thanks for the lives of Zechariah, Elizabeth, and John the Baptist, help us to be attentive to your word and to do your will.
As we rejoice in the birth of John the Baptist, empower us to tell of your love.
Bless, O Lord, all who are baptised and immersed in your presence and power.
Strengthen all who are seeking to dedicate their lives to you.
We pray for all new Christians and all who are growing in the faith.
We pray for all who have hardened their hearts and are deaf to your call.
Lord, you are our strength and salvation:
in your grace, hear our prayer.

God, our Father, we pray for all who are not at peace with themselves or any other; all those who are causing strife and terror.
We remember all whose lives are being spoiled by hatred, or who are seeking revenge.
May they come to know your love and your peace, and seek to show that peace to others.
We pray for peace in our world and in the hearts of all your people.
Lord, you are our strength and salvation:
in your grace, hear our prayer.

God, our Father, we pray for all who have a new member to their family.
We ask your blessing upon the newly born and their homes.
We remember before you those who work in maternity wards and all who care for expectant mothers.
We give you thanks for our own parents and all who love us and care for us.
We ask your blessing upon all children who are unwanted or taken into care.
Lord, you are our strength and salvation:
in your grace, hear our prayer.

God, our Father, we pray for all who have lost a child at birth, or who have lost a child through accident or illness.
We pray for all who would love to have children, but are unable to.
Bless all who are seeking to adopt children and those who foster children.
We pray for all children caught up in war or the violence of our world.
We remember all who are ill, especially [. . .]
Lord, you are our strength and salvation:
in your grace, hear our prayer.

God, our Father, we give you praise and thanks for our lives and for the gift of eternal life.
We pray for our loved ones departed.
We also pray for those who have died this last week and we pray for [. . .]
Merciful Father,
**accept these prayers for the sake of your Son, our Saviour, Jesus Christ.
Amen.**

The peace

The light of the Lord lead you and guide your feet into the way of peace.
The peace of the Lord be always with you.
And also with you.

Blessing

Know that you are in the heart of God;
you dwell in his love and care:
and the blessing of God Almighty,
the Father, the Son and the Holy Spirit,
be upon you and remain with you always.
Amen.

St Peter (and St Paul)

Simon from Bethsaida was a fisherman, like his brother Andrew who introduced him to Jesus. It was Jesus who named him 'Cephas (Peter)' which means 'rock'. In the list of the apostles, Peter is always given the first place. With his fellow fishermen, James and John, Peter was privileged to witness the Transfiguration, the raising of Jairus's daughter, and the Agony in the Garden. It was when Peter acknowledged Jesus as the Christ that Jesus said he would be the rock upon which the Church was built. After the resurrection of Jesus, in Acts, we see Peter in a leadership role.

Saul was a Roman citizen, a Jew and a Pharisee born in Tarsus. He became a persecutor of the Church, and was present at the stoning of Stephen. On his way to Damascus he had a vision of Christ which convinced him of the risen Lord and the Christian Way. He took the name of Paul to show after his baptism that he walked in newness of life. He became known because of his missionary outreach as the 'Apostle to the Gentiles'. Most of the biblical Epistles are from Paul to Christians in some of the places he had visited.

Both Peter and Paul died in Rome about the year 64, though not together nor on the same day.

Readings

Zechariah 4:1-6a,10b-14
Psalm 125
Acts 12:1-11
Matthew 16:13-19

or

Acts 12:1-11
Psalm 125
2 Timothy 4:6-8,17,18
Matthew 16:13-19

St Peter only

Ezekiel 3:22-27
Psalm 125
Acts 12:1-11
Matthew 16:13-19

or

Acts 12:1-11
Psalm 125
1 Peter 2:19-25
Matthew 16:13-19

Opening prayer

Mighty God, you are our Maker.
You are our Saviour.
You are our Guide.
You are here and with us now:
Glory and praise to you, Father, Son and Holy Spirit.

Mighty God, you are our Keeper.
You are our Lover.
You are our Helper.
You are here and with us now:
Glory and praise to you, Father, Son and Holy Spirit.

Intercessions

Praise and thanks to you, O God, for the witness of all your saints.
For all who have inspired us, all who have told of your love.
We thank you for the lives of St Peter and St Paul; for their confessing
that Jesus is the Christ.
Loving God, we ask your blessing and protection upon all who seek to
make your love known, upon all who witness to your saving power.
We remember all Christian missions, all who risk their lives to reveal
your love, those who write and tell us of your presence.
We pray for all preachers of the word, especially [. . .]
God, our Creator:
we ask this in the name of Christ our Lord.

Loving God, we ask your blessing upon the work of the United Nations and all peace-keeping forces.

We remember communities torn apart by hatred, nations that are divided against nations.

We pray for all who are caught in places of dissatisfaction or violence, all who suffer through acts of terrorism.

Strengthen, O Lord, all who seek to live in peace and harmony.

God, our Creator:

we ask this in the name of Christ our Lord.

Loving God, we ask your blessing upon our lives that we may be instruments of your peace.

May we carry peace in our hearts and minds, reveal peace in our homes and live in love and peace with each other, and so reveal you as the God of peace and love.

We ask your blessing upon all care organisations in our community and in the world at large.

We give thanks for all who care for our needs.

We pray especially for […]

God, our Creator:

we ask this in the name of Christ our Lord.

Loving God, we ask your blessing upon all who are ill at this time.

We remember all who are unable to work through their disability,

all who are unable to care for themselves,

all who are terminally ill.

We pray for friends and loved ones who are suffering at this time, especially […]

God, our Creator:

we ask this in the name of Christ our Lord.

Loving God, as we give you thanks for what we have learnt from the lives of St Peter and St Paul and for all who have been faithful labourers in your name:

we remember all who have died witnessing to your love.

We pray for all our loved ones departed and we pray especially today for […]

Merciful Father,

accept these prayers for the sake of your Son, our Saviour, Jesus Christ. Amen.

The peace

Salvation belongs to our God, who will guide us into the way of peace.
The peace of the Lord be always with you.
And also with you.

Blessing

To the One who is our God and our Creator,
to Jesus the Christ who is our Saviour,
to the Holy Spirit who dwells within us,
be all praise and glory for ever:
and the blessing of God Almighty,
the Father, the Son and the Holy Spirit,
be upon you and remain with you always.
Amen.

JULY

St Thomas

St Thomas was also called Didymus, which means a twin. He was a Galilean Jew and one of the twelve apostles. In St John's Gospel, we hear of him encouraging the disciples to go to Judea with Jesus and expressing a willingness to die with him (John 11:16). For some reason Thomas was not with the ten at the resurrection of Jesus. He could not be persuaded it had happened but was only willing to believe if he saw for himself. When Jesus appeared to him a week later, Thomas expressed his faith in the words: 'My Lord and My God!' (John 20:28). Thomas was present at Pentecost but after that little is known about him. However, there is a strong tradition he went to India where he was martyred. His relics were said to be at Mylapore near Madras. An ancient cross marked the place where they were before 394 when they were translated to Edessa. In the ninth century King Alfred sent alms to Rome, and to India for the churches founded by St Thomas and St Bartholomew. When the Portuguese arrived in 1522, St Thomas's tomb was to be seen at Mylapore.

Readings

Habakkuk 2:1-4
Psalm 31:1-6
Ephesians 2:19-22
John 20:24-29

Opening prayer

Lord Jesus Christ, risen from the dead,
you are our Lord and our God.
We believe in you: we seek to know you.

Lord Jesus Christ, appearing to Thomas,
you are our Lord and our God.
We believe in you: we seek to know you.

Lord Jesus Christ, with us in your risen power,
you are our Lord and our God.
We believe in you: we seek to know you.

Lord Jesus Christ, you show us that life is eternal;
you are our Lord and our God.
We believe in you: we seek to know you.

Intercessions

Father, we give you thanks and praise for the resurrection of Christ, your Son, our Lord.
We give thanks for St Thomas and his seeking to know the risen Christ.
We ask you to bless all who preach and teach the power of the resurrection.
We pray for those who are sharing their faith with others and leading them to Christ.
We remember all who are struggling with doubt and darkness.
We pray for all who are seeking to know the risen Lord.
Christ, be known among us,
in your risen power.

Father, we give you thanks for the Church in India and its witness to the risen Lord.
We ask your blessing upon the Church in India today and on its work among the poor.
We pray for the people of India, for their peace and prosperity.
We ask your guidance upon the government of India and all its leaders.
Christ, be known among us,
in your risen power.

Father, we give you thanks for the risen presence of Christ revealed in an earthly home.
Lord, make yourself known to us in our homes, in our fellowship and in the breaking of the bread.
Lord, teach us to be at home with you in our homes. May our homes be where your presence is known.
We remember all who are newly married and those in new homes.
Christ, be known among us,
in your risen power.

Father, we give you thanks for the promise and new hope that is ours through the resurrection.
We pray for all who are discouraged or without hope at this time.
We remember those who are seriously ill and any who are facing death.
We pray for those who are caring for the ill and any who are anxious about loved ones.
We pray especially today for [. . .]
Christ, be known among us,
in your risen power.

Father, we give you thanks for the triumph of Christ over death, and for opening to us the way to glory.
We give thanks for St Thomas and for all who have given their lives in the service of humankind.
We remember our loved ones departed and ask that they may rejoice in the fullness of life eternal.
Merciful Father,
accept these prayers for the sake of your Son, our Saviour, Jesus Christ.
Amen.

The peace

The presence and the power of the risen Lord fill you with joy and peace in believing.
The peace of the Lord be always with you.
And also with you.

Blessing

The risen Christ be with you to protect you
and fill your life with love and joy;
know that you dwell in him and he in you:
and the blessing of God Almighty,
the Father, the Son and the Holy Spirit,
be upon you and remain with you always.
Amen.

St Mary Magdalene

Mary Magdalene was the first person to see the risen Lord, and she went to tell the disciples: it is for this reason she is known as 'the apostle to the Apostles'. It is believed this is the same Mary from 'from whom he had cast out seven demons' (Mark 16:9),and the one who anointed Jesus' feet, wet them with her tears and wiped them dry with her hair (Luke 7:36-38). She is also thought by some parts of the Church to be Mary of Bethany, the sister of Martha, and Lazarus (Matthew 26:6-13, John 11:1-44). She is the patron of repentant sinners, and of the contemplative life.

Readings

Song of Solomon 3:1-4
Psalm 42:1-10
2 Corinthians 5:14-17
John 20:1-2, 11-18

Opening prayer

Jesus Christ, we rejoice in your resurrection.
We are Easter people:
Alleluia is our song.

We praise you for your appearance to Mary Magdalene.
We are Easter people:
Alleluia is our song.

We give thanks for the sending of Mary Magdalene to the disciples.
We are Easter people:
Alleluia is our song.

We believe in the forgiveness of sins and the resurrection of the body.
We are Easter people:
Alleluia is our song.

We rejoice in your presence with us now.
We are Easter people:
Alleluia is our song.

Intercessions

Holy God, Holy and Strong One, with the Church throughout the world and in heaven, we rejoice that the risen Christ appeared to Mary Magdalene.
We rejoice that she 'saw the risen Lord' and went and told the disciples.
We remember all who go out to proclaim the Good News that Christ is risen.
We give thanks for those who taught us the faith and introduced us to the living Lord.
We pray for schools and Sunday schools, for all teachers of religious education.
We ask your blessing upon all who are learning to contemplate and all who live a contemplative life.
We pray for all religious communities, especially those bearing the name of Mary Magdalene.
May Jesus be known to us:
in his risen power.

Holy God, Holy and Strong One, we pray for all who offer hospitality and friendship to others.
We ask your blessing upon those who offer a place of refuge to those who suffer rejection or violence.
We remember those who seek to build up community life and all who work for peace.
We pray for all social services that they may help in the renewing of lives.
May Jesus be known to us:
in his risen power.

Holy God, Holy and Strong One, you bless us with your presence in our homes and in our work.
Open our eyes to your presence and our hearts to your love.
We pray for homes where there is little joy or love.

We remember all families who are struggling at this time.
We pray for all carers and those who show compassion to those in need.
May Jesus be known to us:
in his risen power.

Holy God, Holy and Strong One, may all who are losing heart or who feel discouraged and despondent find new life in Christ, your Son, and in the power of his resurrection.
We bring before you friends and loved ones who are ill, that in you they might find strength and peace. We pray especially for [...]
We pray for all who are terminally ill, for all who are in a hospice or in care; we pray also for their loved ones in this time of anxiety and separation.
We pray for any who are troubled by sin and guilt, that in you they may find peace and forgiveness.
We remember those who have been bereaved this year, especially all who are left on their own and feel lonely or unable to cope.
May Jesus be known to us:
in his risen power.

Holy God, Holy and Strong One, we rejoice in the triumph of Jesus over death and in his appearing to Mary Magdalene.
We pray for all your saints and our loved ones who are departed this life.
May they rejoice with us in the risen Lord and in fullness of life eternal.
Merciful Father,
accept these prayers for the sake of your Son, our Saviour, Jesus Christ. Amen.

The peace

The risen Christ be known among you
and fill your lives and your homes with his joy and his peace.
The peace of the Lord be always with you.
And also with you.

Blessing

The risen Christ scatter the darkness from your hearts and minds,
bringing you his hope and light:
and the blessing of God Almighty,
the Father, the Son and the Holy Spirit,
be upon you and remain with you always.
Amen.

St James

St James is known as 'the Great' to distinguish him from the St James the Less, the son of Alphaeus, who was also a disciple of Jesus. James was the brother of John and they were the fishermen sons of Zebedee. The family lived in Bethsaida. Jesus gave them the nickname 'Boanerges', which means 'Sons of Thunder', because of their fiery temper and impetuosity. With his brother John, and Peter, James was privileged to witness the Transfiguration (Matthew 17:1-8), the raising of Jairus' daughter (Mark 5:35-43), and the Agony in the Garden (Mark 14:32-33). James is not heard of in the Gospels without his brother John. With the apostles he is present at the resurrection and at Pentecost. James is the first of the apostles to be martyred, being killed with the sword at the instigation of Herod Agrippa in the year 44 (Acts 12:1-2). James became associated with Santiago de Compostela where it is believed his relics were interred. Because Compostela became a great place of pilgrimage, James is often depicted as a pilgrim with hat, staff and purse and scallop shell. He is the patron saint of pilgrims.

Readings

Jeremiah 45:1-5
Psalm 126
Acts 11:27–12:2
Matthew 20:20-28

or

Acts 11:27–12:2
Psalm 126
2 Corinthians 4:7-15
Matthew 20:20-28

Opening prayer

Lord, as you called James the fisherman,
open our ears to your call:
and our hearts to your love.

In our daily lives,
open our ears to your call:
and our hearts to your love.

In our places of work,
open our ears to your call:
and our hearts to your love.

In the cries of the needy,
open our ears to your call:
and our hearts to your love.

In our homes and through our loved ones,
open our ears to your call:
and our hearts to your love.

Intercessions

God, our Father, we give thanks and praise for St James, for his presence at the raising of the daughter of Jairus, for his seeing the transfiguration of Jesus and for his witness to the resurrection.
We pray for all who seek to serve you and to share in the work of salvation.
We bring before you all who proclaim the gospel in word, or who witness by their lives.
We ask your blessing upon all places of pilgrimage and all pilgrim people.
We pray for Santiago de Compostela and all churches dedicated in the name of St James.
May we, Father, have a share in bringing in your kingdom on earth.
May your kingdom come on earth:
as it is in heaven.

God, our Father, we ask your blessing upon all leaders of peoples and nations: we pray for Elizabeth, our Queen, and for all the royal family, for our Prime Minister and Parliament.
We ask your guidance upon the world of commerce and all who work in industry.

We remember those whose work is wearisome or unfulfilling and those who are unable to work.
We pray for all who work among and care for the unemployed.
May your kingdom come on earth:
as it is in heaven.

God, our Father, we ask your blessing upon our homes, our loved ones and our friends.
We pray for all who help to build up community life and bring people together.
We pray for schools, colleges and universities, and all who influence the minds of others.
In our area, we pray especially for [...]
May your kingdom come on earth:
as it is in heaven.

God, our Father, we ask your blessing upon all who are suffering in body, mind or spirit.
We pray for all displaced persons, all refugees and those who have been separated from loved ones.
We remember all who suffer from prejudice or wrong judgements.
We pray for all who are ill, at home or in hospital, and all who have been injured this week: we pray especially for [...]
May your kingdom come on earth:
as it is in heaven.

God, our Father, we ask your blessing upon the souls of the departed.
We remember all who have died as martyrs and those who have given their lives in the care and service of others.
We give thanks for the witness and life of St James.
We pray for loved ones departed and especially for [...]
Merciful Father,
accept these prayers for the sake of your Son, our Saviour, Jesus Christ. Amen.

The peace

To those whom he calls he gives the presence and power of his Spirit
and his peace.
The peace of the Lord be always with you.
And also with you.

Blessing

All power belongs to God.
May he raise you up
to live in his presence:
and the blessing of God Almighty,
the Father, the Son and the Holy Spirit,
be upon you and remain with you always.
Amen.

AUGUST

6 AUGUST

The Transfiguration of Our Lord

The Transfiguration is recorded in the first three Gospels (Matthew 17:1-8; Mark 9:2-8; Luke 9:28-36). St Peter refers to it in his Second Letter (2 Peter 1:16-18). However, this is an experience that the disciples must have found hard to put into words because it describes a vision of Jesus as he truly is; it is full of mystery and glory. The Transfiguration follows not long after the declaration that Jesus is the Messiah, the Christ, at Caesarea Philippi. It comes before the time of his suffering, leading to his death, followed by the resurrection and ascension. It is like a foretaste of what the disciples will experience. It is full of ancient symbolism, showing Jesus fulfils the Law (Moses) and the Prophets (Elijah). The shining cloud is a sign of God's presence and the voice was like the voice of God heard on the mountain by Moses and Elijah. The voice is for the disciples' sake and it affirms 'This is my Son, the Beloved; listen to him!' (Mark 9:7). Though it is said they were filled with 'fear', this word can also be translated as 'wonder and awe'.

Readings

Daniel 7:9, 10, 13, 14
Psalm 97
2 Peter 1:16-19
Luke 9:28-36

Opening prayer

Lord God, touch our lives with your glory.
Lord, in your grace and goodness:
grant us a glimpse of your glory.

Touch our eyes that we may see your presence.
May your kingdom come on earth:
as it is in heaven.

Touch our hearts that we may know your love.
May your kingdom come on earth:
as it is in heaven.

Touch our relationships that there we may know you.
May your kingdom come on earth:
as it is in heaven.

Touch our world that it may reveal your love.
May your kingdom come on earth:
as it is in heaven.

Intercessions

Lord, in your Glory, transfigure the Church, that it may radiate your presence, reveal your love and show forth your glory.
May our church buildings be a sign of your presence among us.
May all who are Christians show your acceptance and forgiveness towards others.
We ask your blessing upon our church and all who minister within it.
Lord, may we know you:
and live to your glory.

Lord, in your Glory, transfigure our world, that we may show respect for all your creatures.
We pray that we may care for the earth, above all financial gain.
We ask your blessing upon all who seek to free the world of pollution and to repair damaged areas.
We pray for all conservation agencies and for the World Wildlife Fund.
We remember today all who lost their lives and those who have suffered through the dropping of the atomic bomb on Hiroshima.
Lord, may we know you:
and live to your glory.

Lord, in your Glory, transfigure our homes that they may reveal the brightness and peace of your presence.
We ask your blessing upon all with whom we share our lives and our daily work.

We pray that councils and governments may seek to provide homes for the poor and needy.

We remember all who are living in crowded accommodation or in hostels.

We pray for all who have left home and feel lost and lonely.

We give you thanks for all who have enriched our lives by their goodness.

Lord, may we know you:

and live to your glory.

Lord, in your Glory, transfigure our hospitals and care homes.

We pray for all who seek healing and relief from pain.

We remember all who await a doctor's diagnosis or an operation.

We pray for all who fear the future and those who need help and support.

We remember friends and loved ones in illness, especially [. . .]

Lord, may we know you:

and live to your glory.

Lord, in your Glory, transfigure all who have passed beyond death into the fullness of life in your kingdom.

We pray for our teachers, benefactors and loved ones who are departed, that they may rejoice in your glory, in the fullness of your kingdom.

We pray today especially for [. . .]

Merciful Father,

accept these prayers for the sake of your Son, our Saviour, Jesus Christ. Amen.

The peace

The glory of the Lord fills the heavens and the earth. Live in his glory and his peace.

The peace of the Lord be always with you.

And also with you.

Blessing

May God, our Father, open your eyes to see his glory
in all people, in all creatures
and in all that he has made:
and the blessing of God Almighty,
the Father, the Son and the Holy Spirit,
be upon you and remain with you always.
Amen.

The Blessed Virgin Mary

Nothing is known for sure about the parentage of the Blessed Virgin Mary. Tradition has given the names of Anne (Anna, or Hannah) and Joachim to her parents, but this is from the second-century Apocryphal Gospel of St James and is heavily based on the story of Hannah and the birth of Samuel. We know only Mary's name which is Miriam in Hebrew. We know that she had a relative called Elizabeth who was married to Zechariah. St Luke tells us that Mary was a young Jewish woman living in Nazareth and was engaged to Joseph. This festival marks a new start as we move from the Old Testament to the New. In Mary, God's purpose of love to send his Son into the world sees its earthly beginning. Today we remember her death and her entering into the glory of heaven.

Readings

Isaiah 61:10, 11 *or* Revelation 11:19–12:6, 10
Psalm 45:10-17
Galatians 4:4-7
Luke 1:46-55

Opening prayer

Father, for the birth of the Virgin Mary:
we praise and glorify your name.

We give you thanks and praise:
we praise and glorify your name.

For the visitation of the angel to her:
we praise and glorify your name.

For her willing obedience to your call:
we praise and glorify your name.

For the overshadowing of the Holy Spirit:
we praise and glorify your name.

For the birth of Christ our Lord:
we praise and glorify your name.

For Mary's loving care of Jesus:
we praise and glorify your name.

For Mary in the glory of heaven:
we praise and glorify your name.

For Christ's presence with us now:
we praise and glorify your name.

Intercessions

Loving God, we thank you for Mary, for her obedience and her joy.
We rejoice that, through Mary, our Saviour came to dwell among us.
May we learn the obedience of Mary, serving you with joy and accepting Jesus into our lives.
We pray for all churches and communities dedicated in the name of the Virgin Mary.
We ask your blessing on all who quietly witness to your presence, through faithfulness in prayer.
We pray for the work of the Mothers' Union and all who support family life.
God of love, God of glory:
Be known among us.

Loving God, we ask your blessing upon all who care for homeless or unwanted children, and on all children taken into care.
We pray for social workers and adoption agencies.
We remember the street children of the world and all who are in areas of violence or disaster.
We pray for the work of Save the Children, The Children's Society, and the NSPCC.
God of love, God of glory:
Be known among us.

Loving God, we give thanks for the love of our homes.
We pray for our parents and for all who have accepted us and cared for us.
We ask your blessing upon all who are separated from loved ones and on all who are lonely.
We pray for all who help others to live in their own homes.
God of love, God of glory:
Be known among us.

Loving God, we remember all who are hungry for love and all who long to be needed.
We pray for all expectant mothers and all who have gone into labour.
We ask your blessing on all who have a new addition to their family.
We pray for all children waiting to be adopted.
We remember all who are in hospital and loved ones who are anxious.
We pray especially for [. . .]
God of love, God of glory:
Be known among us.

Loving God, we give thanks for Jesus' life and home in Nazareth and for Mary and Joseph.
Lord God, you came to dwell among us, that we might share in your kingdom of heaven.
Bless our friends and loved ones who are departed this life with the gift of life and love eternal.
We pray especially for [. . .]
Merciful Father,
accept these prayers for the sake of your Son, our Saviour, Jesus Christ. Amen.

The peace

Through the obedience of Mary, God has sent his Son to dwell among us that we may know his love and his peace.
The peace of the Lord be always with you.
And also with you.

Blessing

God give you grace to follow the example of Mary
and to welcome the Christ into your life and home.
Know that the Holy Spirit overshadows you and protects you:
and the blessing of God Almighty,
the Father, the Son and the Holy Spirit,
be upon you and remain with you always.
Amen.

St Bartholomew

Bartholomew was a Jew from Galilee, whom it is believed was also called Nathanael. In St John's Gospel, when Jesus called Philip from Bethsaida, the city of Andrew and Peter, Philip went and called Nathanael. But Nathanael doubted that anything good could come out of Nazareth! Philip simply said, 'Come and see.' When he came, Jesus said of him, 'Here is truly an Israelite in whom there is no deceit!' (John 1:43-51). In the lists of the apostles, Philip and Bartholomew are linked together (Matthew 10:3; Mark 3:18). It could be that Bartholomew is a second name meaning 'Son of Tholomai or Ptolemy'. Outside the Gospels little is known of Bartholomew for certain. Tradition says he preached the gospel in India and Armenia, where he was martyred by being flayed alive. His name has become associated with medicine and hospitals.

Readings

Isaiah 43:8-13
Psalm 145:1-7
Acts 5:12-16
Luke 22:24-30

or

Acts 5:12-16
Psalm 145:1-7
1 Corinthians 4:9-15
Luke 22:24-30

Opening prayer

Christ, you called Bartholomew.
As you have called us:
make us worthy of our calling.

Christ, you empowered him to be an apostle.
As you have called us:
make us worthy of our calling.

Christ, as an apostle you sent him out.
As you have called us:
make us worthy of our calling.

Christ, he was full of your Holy Spirit.
As you have called us:
make us worthy of our calling.

Christ, he told of you and was a witness of your resurrection.
As you have called us:
make us worthy of our calling.

Intercessions

Father, your Son called Bartholomew to leave the past behind him and to follow as a disciple.
He called him to be an apostle and to go out and proclaim the Good News.
As we give thanks for the life of Bartholomew, we pray for those whom he calls today to be his disciples.
We ask your blessing upon all who study the Scriptures, all who produce Bibles and commentaries, those who preach the word and those who administer the sacraments.
We pray for all who are zealous in the faith, that they may be directed into the ways of peace and gentleness.
Loving God:
hear us and help us.

Father, your Son at Easter breathed on the disciples his gifts of the Spirit and of peace.
We pray for all who strive to bring peace to our lives and to the world.
We remember the Jewish people and pray for peace in the Holy Land.
We ask your blessing on all areas where there is conflict and unrest at this time, especially [. . .]

May we have peace in our hearts and minds and show forth your peace to the world.
Loving God:
hear us and help us.

Father, your Son called around him a company of friends. We ask your blessing upon our friends and families.
We pray for all who enrich our lives through art and music, through writing and publishing.
We remember those who work in the media and all who influence our minds.
We pray for all who feel friendless and all who live in places of fear or dullness.
Loving God:
hear us and help us.

Father, your Son sent out your disciples to preach and heal the sick. We pray today for St Bartholomew's Hospital and all who care for the ill, especially those with cancer or in need of cardiac care.
We pray for their loved ones, the doctors, surgeons, nurses and all the hospital staff and all who are a calming influence.
We ask your blessing upon all who are in training to be doctors, nurses or paramedics.
We pray for friends and loved ones who are ill. We pray especially for [...]
Loving God:
hear us and help us.

Father, your Son came to earth that we might share in your kingdom in heaven.
He became human that we might share in the divine.
We pray for all our loved ones departed: may they, with Bartholomew, rejoice in the fullness of eternal life.
We pray especially for [...]
Merciful Father,
accept these prayers for the sake of your Son, our Saviour, Jesus Christ. Amen.

The peace

The peace of Christ be in your hearts and minds, in your lives and homes.
The peace of the Lord be always with you.
And also with you.

Blessing

Go out in the power of the Spirit,
rejoicing in the resurrection.
Live and work to Christ's praise and glory:
and the blessing of God Almighty,
the Father, the Son and the Holy Spirit,
be upon you and remain with you always.
Amen.

SEPTEMBER

Holy Cross Day

The Holy Cross is the icon of God's love for his creation and his giving of himself for us. The cross became the main symbol of Christianity. Due to the Emperor Constantine's adoption of Christianity, the age of the Roman Empire's persecutions of the Church ended in the early fourth century. Constantine's mother, Helena, went on pilgrimage to the Holy Land in 326. There she founded the building of a basilica on the Mount of Olives and another at Bethlehem. While overseeing excavations in Jerusalem, she is said to have discovered the holy cross. She then caused the basilica of the Holy Sepulchre to be built on the site. It was dedicated this day in the year 335.

Readings

Numbers 21:4-9
Psalm 22:23-28
Philippians 2:6-11
John 3:13-17

Opening prayer

Christ, who died for us:
help us to live for you.

By your rejection and scorning,
Christ, who died for us:
help us to live for you.

By your scourging and agony,
Christ, who died for us:
help us to live for you.

By your sacred wounds,
Christ, who died for us:
help us to live for you.

By your hunger and thirst,
Christ, who died for us:
help us to live for you.

By your death and burial,
Christ, who died for us:
help us to live for you.

By your victory over death,
Christ, who died for us:
help us to live for you.

Intercessions

God of love, we thank you for the pilgrimage and discovery of the
Cross by St Helena.
We ask your blessing upon all pilgrims and those who look after sacred
sites; we pray especially for the Holy Land and for its peace.
We remember all who suffer for their faith, all who are mocked, all
who are treated with violence and any whose lives are endangered.
God of love, be to them a strength and shield.
We pray for all who have lost faith through the wickedness of others.
Lord of the Cross and of glory:
hear us and help us.

God of love, we remember before you all who suffer from prejudice or
hatred.
We pray for all innocent sufferers caught up in acts of violence or war.
We ask your blessing upon all whose lives have been corrupted or
destroyed by the greed or evil of others.
We pray for all who seek peace and unity in our world.
Lord of the Cross and of glory:
hear us and help us.

God of love, we rejoice before you in our loved ones. Help us to be ever
mindful of all they have sacrificed and done for us, and all the joy they
bring to us.

God, as we grow in love for each other, may we grow in love for you.
We pray for all whose love has been betrayed or rejected, and for those who are afraid to love.
We ask your blessing upon our homes and on all who are dear to us.
Lord of the Cross and of glory:
hear us and help us.

God of love, we remember before you all who are lonely.
We ask your blessing upon all who are broken in body, mind or spirit, on all who are despairing or despondent.
We remember those who patiently bear their sorrows and pain, and those who cry out in their need.
We pray for all who are ill and especially for [. . .]
Lord of the Cross and of glory:
hear us and help us.

Loving God, we give thanks for the triumph of Our Lord over sin and death.
In his death, he has destroyed death.
In his rising, he has opened to us the gate of glory.
We ask your blessing upon all who have died for their faith, and all who have sacrificed their lives for others. We pray for all the departed and especially for [. . .]
Merciful Father,
accept these prayers for the sake of your Son, our Saviour, Jesus Christ. Amen.

The peace

May you find in Christ crucified
the forgiveness of your sins,
the hope of life eternal,
and his abiding presence and peace.
The peace of the Lord be always with you.
And also with you.

Blessing

Christ of the cross deliver you from all evil,
keep you firm in your love for him:
and the blessing of God Almighty,
the Father, the Son and the Holy Spirit,
be upon you and remain with you always.
Amen.

21 SEPTEMBER

St Matthew

In the Gospel bearing his name, Matthew is shown as a tax-collector (9:9). Mark and Luke's Gospels call him Levi (Mark 2:13-17; Luke 5:27-32). This name implies he was descended from the priestly family of Levites. By working for the enemy of occupation and collecting taxes from his people, he was not only despised, he was barred from the synagogue as unclean, and seen as a quisling. Yet Jesus called Matthew and ate with his friends, scandalising those who lived by the letter of the law. When Jesus called him, it was not for what he was but who he could become. In leaving his past behind, newness of life became possible. The accountant became the one to give an account of Jesus. As an educated man, he had the skill to write as an eye witness to the life of Jesus. As a Jew, Matthew wrote his Gospel in order to convince the Jews and showed how Jesus fulfilled all the Old Testament prophecies, and therefore must be the Messiah. In art the symbol of St Matthew is that of a man, remembering his depiction of Jesus born of woman and with a human family tree.

Readings

Proverbs 3:13-18
Psalm 119:65-72
2 Corinthians 4:1-6
Matthew 9:9-13

Opening prayer

Lord Jesus, as you called Matthew,
open our ears to your call:
open our hearts to your love.

As Matthew left off collecting taxes,
open our ears to your call:
open our hearts to your love.

As he left all and followed you,
open our ears to your call:
open our hearts to your love.

As he listened to your word,
open our ears to your call:
open our hearts to your love.

As he went out in mission,
open our ears to your call:
open our hearts to your love.

As he witnessed your death and resurrection,
open our ears to your call:
open our hearts to your love.

As he told of you in his Gospel,
open our ears to your call:
open our hearts to your love.

Intercessions

Lord of life and love, we give you thanks for the calling of Matthew
from collecting taxes to be one to seek to win his people for Christ.
We rejoice that the accountant gave such a good account of the life
of Jesus.
We ask your blessing upon those who are called to proclaim the gospel
and to give account of you.
We pray for all preachers and evangelists and all who seek to interpret
the Gospels for us.
We pray for all who are called to witness by their lives to your power
and your love.
We ask that we also may help to bring others to know you and love you.
Lord, as you have called us:
make us worthy of our calling.

Lord of life and love, we ask your blessing upon all who seek to fulfil
their calling in life.

We pray for those who seek to build up relationships and communities and lead us into ways of peace.
We remember those who encourage us all to love and care for your world.
We pray for those whose calling is frustrated by illness, by war, or by the prejudice of others.
Lord, as you have called us:
make us worthy of our calling.

Lord of life and love, as you have given us life, may we learn to live to your glory and in love of you.
We ask your blessing upon the communities and organisations to which we belong.
We pray for all who maintain and look after our streets and our safety.
We ask your blessing upon all who provide us with food and security.
We pray for our own families and friends.
Lord, as you have called us:
make us worthy of our calling.

Lord of life and love, we give thanks for the healing and peace that is offered through the Gospels.
We pray for all who work in the healing professions, and for our own doctors [. . .]
We remember all who are denied healing and help through poverty or war.
We ask your blessing upon all who are caring for a loved one who is terminally ill, and for the work of hospices.
We pray especially for [. . .]
Lord, as you have called us:
make us worthy of our calling.

We give thanks for St Matthew's Gospel and its telling of your love and of the resurrection.
We give thanks for eternal life where sorrow and pain are no more.
We pray for all who have touched our lives and are now in life eternal.
We pray today especially for [. . .]
Merciful Father,
accept these prayers for the sake of your Son, our Saviour, Jesus Christ. Amen.

The peace

Love the Lord your God, with all your heart and mind and strength,
and tell of his love and peace.
The peace of the Lord be always with you.
And also with you.

Blessing

The Lord God fill your life
with his loving presence
and keep you from harm:
and the blessing of God Almighty,
the Father, the Son and the Holy Spirit,
be upon you and remain with you always.
Amen.

St Michael and All Angels

St Michael is one of the three archangels mentioned in the Scriptures. His name means 'who is like God'. He is portrayed as the protector of Israel and leader of the armies of God (Daniel 10:13ff; 12:1). In the book of Revelation he is described as the slayer of the dragon (Revelation 12:7-9) and in Jude (verse 9) he is shown as contending with the devil for the body of Moses. He is seen as the protector of Christians from the Evil One, especially at death. Gabriel ('Strength of God') is the one who announces to Mary what God seeks of her in the birth of Jesus. Raphael ('Healing of God') is depicted in the book of Tobit as the one who heals Tobit's blindness. In the fifth century a basilica was dedicated near Rome to St Michael on 30 September with celebrations beginning on the eve; therefore this day, 29 September, was chosen to remember the angelic hosts.

Readings

Genesis 28:10-17
Psalm 103:19-22
Revelation 12:7-12
John 1:47-51

or

Revelation 12:7-12
Psalm 103:19-22
Hebrews 1:5-14
John 1:47-51

Opening prayer

Good Lord, as angels foretold your birth,
give your angels charge over us:
to guard us in all our ways.

Good Lord, as angels proclaimed the good news to the shepherds,
give your angels charge over us:
to guard us in all our ways.

Good Lord, as angels ministered to you in the wilderness,
give your angels charge over us:
to guard us in all our ways.

Good Lord, as angels announced your resurrection to Mary Magdalene,
give your angels charge over us:
to guard us in all our ways.

Good Lord, as angels were seen at your ascension,
give your angels charge over us:
to guard us in all our ways.

Intercessions

Gracious God, we give thanks for St Michael and all Angels.
May we be aware of all the messengers and messages you send to us.
As the angels serve and worship you in heaven, strengthen us and
your whole Church to serve you here on earth.
We pray for all churches dedicated in the names of the archangels and
angels.
We ask your blessing upon us as we worship, seeking to share in the
worship of angels.
Lord, make us aware of your angels:
teach us to hear and obey you.

Gracious God, when the angels told of the birth of your Son, they sang
'Glory to God and peace on earth'.
We ask that we may glorify you in our daily work and lives.
We pray for peace in our hearts, minds and world.
We ask your blessing upon the United Nations and all peace-keeping
forces.
We remember all who work for peace in our communities and all who
care for the earth.
Lord, make us aware of your angels:
teach us to hear and obey you.

Gracious God, as the angel Gabriel visited the Blessed Virgin in her home, may we be aware of all who in their lives declare your presence and love. Through hospitality may we entertain those who visit us as angelic messengers.
We ask your blessing upon our homes, loved ones and friends.
Lord, make us aware of your angels:
teach us to hear and obey you.

Gracious God, as an angel appeared to St Paul in prison, loosed his chains and brought him to freedom, we pray for all who seek to bring freedom to others.
We pray for the work of Amnesty International and all who care for prisoners.
We remember all who are imprisoned unjustly or through the wickedness of others.
We ask your blessing upon all who are made to work for very little reward.
We pray for all who are ill and we remember today [...]
Lord, make us aware of your angels:
teach us to hear and obey you.

Gracious God, as angels spoke of the resurrection, we give thanks that, in you, life is eternal.
We rejoice with St Michael, angels and archangels and all your saints.
We remember loved ones departed and we pray especially today for [...]
Merciful Father,
accept these prayers for the sake of your Son, our Saviour, Jesus Christ. Amen.

The peace

At the birth of Christ, the angels sang 'Glory to God in the highest and peace on earth'.
The peace of the Lord be always with you.
And also with you.

Blessing

Remember to show your love to strangers
for thereby some have entertained angels unawares:
and the blessing of God Almighty,
the Father, the Son and the Holy Spirit,
be upon you and remain with you always.
Amen.

OCTOBER

St Luke

Luke is the only New Testament writer who is a Gentile and not a Jew. He was a Greek and a physician (Colossians 4:14). He travelled with St Paul on some of his missionary journeys of which he kept a record (Acts 16:11; 20:13; 27–28). For two years he was St Paul's companion when he was under house arrest in Caesarea. He is the author of the third Gospel and of the Acts of the Apostles. He is a careful historian and writes good Greek. He seldom quotes from the Old Testament and gives Hebrew words their Greek equivalent. His Gospel reveals his own compassion and interest in healing. He wrote for the Gentile world and sought to show Jesus as the Saviour of the world. Both his books are addressed to Theophilus, whose name means 'One who loves God'. He shows a great artistry in words and it is probably for this reason he is traditionally called an artist. He is the patron saint of surgeons, doctors and artists. In art the symbol for St Luke is an ox, a symbol of service and strength but also of sacrifice.

Readings

Isaiah 35:3-6 *or* Acts 16:6-12a
Psalm 147:1-7
2 Timothy 4:5-17
Luke 10:1-9

Opening prayer

Lord who loves us,
Lord who listens to us,
heal us and help us:
and draw us to yourself.

Lord of the helpless,
Lord of the hopeless,
heal us and help us:
and draw us to yourself.

Lord of the storm-tossed,
Lord of the seekers,
heal us and help us:
and draw us to yourself.

Intercessions

God of grace, we thank you for the life of St Luke, and the Good News
he proclaimed in his Gospel.
We give thanks for his writing of the Acts of the Apostles and for his
companionship of St Paul.
We ask your blessing upon all who teach and preach of your love and
saving power.
We pray for all those who are teaching and learning religious education;
we remember all theological colleges.
We remember those who have shared their faith with us and taught us
of your love.
We pray for all who go out in mission and those who support them in
their work.
God of healing and renewal:
hear us and help us.

God of grace, we give thanks for the artistry of St Luke.
We ask your blessing upon artists, writers and craftspeople, upon all
who beautify our world.
We remember architects and gardeners, musicians and sculptors.
We pray for all whose lives are surrounded with squalor or drabness
and all who have lost any sense of beauty.
God of healing and renewal:
hear us and help us.

God of grace, we thank you for all who have supported our lives by
their love and generosity.
We pray for friends, teachers and loved ones, all who have stood by us
in difficult times.
We ask your blessing upon all who are lonely and without help or
support.

We pray for all befriending agencies, carers and the social services.
God of healing and renewal:
hear us and help us.

God of grace, as we remember that St Luke was a doctor, we pray for all in the healing professions.
We ask your blessing upon nurses and doctors, upon paramedics and ambulance men and women.
We pray for those who work in hospitals and all home visitors.
We pray for all who are ill at this time. We remember especially [...]
God of healing and renewal:
hear us and help us.

God of grace, we give thanks for the gift of eternal life.
We rejoice in the fellowship of St Luke, your saints and the faithful departed.
We pray today especially for [...]
Merciful Father,
**accept these prayers for the sake of your Son, our Saviour, Jesus Christ.
Amen.**

The peace

Salvation belongs to our God, who will guide us into the ways of peace.
The peace of the Lord be always with you.
And also with you.

Blessing

To the one who sits on the throne and to Christ our Lord
be glory, honour, might and blessing:
and the blessing of God Almighty,
the Father, the Son and the Holy Spirit,
be upon you and remain with you always.
Amen.

St Simon and St Jude

Simon and Jude were both apostles. Simon is described as a 'Canaanite'; St Luke describes him as a 'Zealot' which probably implies that he belonged to a nationalistic sect before Jesus called him. Simon is heard of no more after Pentecost.

Jude is usually identified also as Thaddaeus, and as Jude, one of the brothers of James. Like Simon, little is known about him after Pentecost. Because Jude's name is very like Judas, very few prayers were made to him. And because of this he became the patron saint of 'lost causes' and 'dire circumstances'. Tradition has the two saints preaching together and both being martyred in Persia.

Readings

Isaiah 28:14-16
Psalm 119:89-96
Ephesians 2:19-22
John 15:17-27

Opening prayer

Christ of the weak ones,
Christ of the weary ones,
come to us in your love:
and be our hope and strength.

Christ of the lonely ones,
Christ of the lost ones,
come to us in your love:
and be our hope and strength.

Christ on the cross,
Christ of the resurrection,
come to us in your love:
and be our hope and strength.

Intercessions

Loving Father, we give you thanks for the lives and witness of St Simon and St Jude.
May we seek to know your gospel, to live your gospel and to proclaim your gospel.
Bless your Church in its outreach, in its working for your kingdom, in its revealing your love.
We pray for the Church's work among all who have lost their way in a secular society.
We remember the work of the Church among outcasts and refugees.
God, our hope and our strength:
hear us as we pray.

Loving Father, bless all who work with compassion for the freedom of all humankind.
We pray for all who seek to bring liberty to captives and all who work for justice and peace.
We remember all who are used as slave labour, or who are forced to work in dangerous conditions. May we all remember life cannot be bought or sold.
We pray for fair trade among peoples and nations.
God, our hope and our strength:
hear us as we pray.

Loving Father, we give thanks for all who share their love and peace with us.
We ask your blessing upon our families and friends and upon all who build up community life.
We pray for our schools and all who influence our lives through the media.
We remember all who work in conservation and deal gently with the earth.
God, our hope and our strength:
hear us as we pray.

Loving Father, we remember all whose lives are restricted through disabilities, or circumstance.
We pray for all whose vision is seriously threatened and for the work of Sightsavers, and that of ophthalmic surgeons.

We think with compassion of all who suffer from depression or self-doubt, and any who may be tempted to end their lives.
We remember also friends and loved ones who are ill and all who are in hospital; we pray especially for [...]
God, our hope and our strength:
hear us as we pray.

Loving Father, may we rejoice in the resurrection of our Lord and the fullness of life which is eternal.
We give thanks for all your saints, remembering today especially St Simon and St Jude.
We pray for our loved ones who are departed, especially for [...]:
may they know the light and love of your presence.
Merciful Father,
accept these prayers for the sake of your Son, our Saviour, Jesus Christ. Amen.

The peace

The power of God is able to meet all our needs.
The presence of God is always with us.
The peace of God is offered to us.
The peace of the Lord be always with you.
And also with you.

Blessing

To the King of kings and Lord of lords
be all honour, glory and power,
for ever and ever:
and the blessing of God Almighty,
the Father, the Son and the Holy Spirit,
be upon you and remain with you always.
Amen.

NOVEMBER

All Souls

This day, the day after All Saints, is when we remember all the Faithful Departed. Though prayers for the dead were inscribed on some of the catacombs in Rome, the Church was slow to add a liturgical day for remembering the dead. It began in the eleventh century in the Abbey at Cluny, near Dijon in Burgundy, as a way of praying for monks of the past who had died and it was decreed that the day following All Saints should be the day to do this. By the thirteenth century it was being observed throughout the Western Church. Although it did not survive in the Reformation in the Church of England, it was reintroduced in the 1928 Book of Common Prayer. It is a day when people are able to express their love and their grief for the loss of loved ones and people who have inspired them. It also acknowledges that the Church in Heaven and on earth is one.

Readings

Lamentations 3:17-26, 31-33 *or* Wisdom 3:1-9
Psalm 23 *or* 27:1-6
Romans 5:5-11 *or* 1 Peter 1:3-9
John 5:19-25 *or* John 6:37-40

Opening prayer

God our Creator, giver of life and life eternal,
keep us in your love:
and in life which is eternal.

Christ our Redeemer, opening to us the way to glory,
keep us in your love:
and in life which is eternal.

Holy Spirit, Breath of Life, reviving us,
keep us in your love:
and in life which is eternal.

Blessed Trinity, about us and within us,
keep us in your love:
and in life which is eternal.

Intercessions

God of life, we thank you for life eternal.
We rejoice in the heritage of holy men and women who have preached the word.
We give thanks for all who translated and provided us with the Scriptures,
for those who built our churches and cathedrals,
for all who have taught us the faith.
We ask your blessing upon all who continue this work today.
Give rest, O Christ,
to your servants with your saints.

God of life, we thank you for life eternal.
We give thanks for those who have cared for the earth,
those who have tended our fields and shaped our landscape,
those who have built our towns and cities and laid out our roads,
those who have cared for the creatures of the earth and left us a rich inheritance.
We ask your blessing upon all who continue this work today.
Give rest, O Christ,
to your servants with your saints.

God of life, we thank you for life eternal.
We thank you for our ancestors,
those who shaped our lives and provided for us to be here.
We remember their joys and their sorrows and the love they shared.
We remember all who are bereaved and grieving at this time, especially
[. . .]
Give rest, O Christ,
to your servants with your saints.

God of life, we thank you for life eternal.
We give thanks for all who have made sacrifices for others,
for all who have done research into medicines and healing.

We pray for all who care for the grieving and the dying.
We pray for the work of local hospitals and hospices.
Give rest, O Christ,
to your servants with your saints.

God of life, we thank you for life eternal.
We ask your blessing upon all who are departed from us.
(In a moment of silence we remember our own loved ones departed.)
We pray for all who have died this year, especially [...]
May they all know the joy and fullness of your presence in eternal life.
Merciful Father,
accept these prayers for the sake of your Son, our Saviour, Jesus Christ.
Amen.

The peace

In the compassion of our God, the dawn from on high will break upon us.
To shine on those who dwell in darkness and the shadow of death, and
to guide our feet into the way of peace.
The peace of the Lord be always with you.
And also with you.

Blessing

Know in your heart and mind
that neither life nor death
can separate us from the love of God in Christ Jesus:
and the blessing of God Almighty,
the Father, the Son and the Holy Spirit,
be upon you and remain with you always.
Amen.

St Andrew

St Andrew was the brother of Peter. Their home was at Capernaum. Andrew was a disciple of John the Baptist before becoming an apostle of Jesus. In all the Gospels his name is listed with his brother and with James and John, the sons of Zebedee. He is especially noted for bringing a young boy to the attention of Jesus at the feeding of the 5000 (John 6:1-14). When the Greeks wanted to see Jesus they told Philip, and Philip told Andrew who again brought them to Jesus (John 12:20-23). It is not certain where he died or when; the most ancient tradition links him with Greece. As early as the first half of the seventh century Hexham and Rochester churches were dedicated to him. Tradition tells that in the eighth century St Rule came to Scotland and brought some of Andrew's relics with him. He stopped in Fife and built a church in a place that is now called St Andrews. This became a centre of evangelism and pilgrimage. For this reason St Andrew became the patron saint of Scotland; he is also the patron saint of Russia.

Readings

Isaiah 52:7-10
Psalm 19:1-6
Romans 10:12-18
Matthew 4:18-22

Opening prayer

Lord, touch our eyes to see you in all people.
As you have called us,
Lord, make us worthy of our calling.

Lord, touch our ears to hear your call in all encounters.
As you have called us,
Lord, make us worthy of our calling.

Lord, touch our hearts to love you through our homes.
As you have called us,
Lord, make us worthy of our calling.

Lord, touch our lives with your glory that is all about us.
As you have called us,
Lord, make us worthy of our calling.

Lord, touch our wills to obey and serve you with joy.
As you have called us,
Lord, make us worthy of our calling.

Intercessions

We rejoice, O Lord, in St Andrew hearing your call and serving you faithfully.
We ask your blessing upon all who are dedicated in the name of St Andrew: places, churches and people.
We pray for St Andrews in Scotland and for its university.
We pray for the various churches in Scotland and Russia and pray we may all realise we have one faith and we worship One Lord, One God.
We remember especially today all who are providing Bibles and scriptures for people.
God, who calls us to serve you:
hear our prayer.

We remember the countries of Russia and Scotland and pray for their leaders.
We pray for the Scottish parliament and its contribution to the diversity of our nation.
We remember especially all who work for justice and care.
We pray for all who are seeking to fulfil their purpose in life; we pray for schools, colleges and universities.
We pray for all who work upon the sea and all who farm and care for the land.
May we all use the resources of the world with care and respect.
God, who calls us to serve you:
hear our prayer.

We give thanks for our homes and our loved ones, for all who have enriched us by their love and generosity.
We pray for those who have long been our friends and rejoice in their support.
We remember those who are without friends or who are separated from them.
We ask your blessing upon all who are lonely and all who cannot cope on their own.
God, who calls us to serve you:
hear our prayer.

We ask your blessing upon all who are finding life difficult through oppression or harsh laws.
We pray for those who are struggling through debt, poverty or homelessness.
We remember all who are ill and we pray especially at this time for […]
We pray for all who feel their abilities are being wasted or thwarted through circumstance.
May we know that in whatever circumstance we find ourselves, God still loves us and calls us to love him.
God, who calls us to serve you:
hear our prayer.

As we rejoice in the life of St Andrew, may we remember we are called to life which is eternal.
We remember friends and loved ones who are departed from us, praying especially for […]
May we all share in your abiding love and in the fullness of life eternal.
Merciful Father,
accept these prayers for the sake of your Son, our Saviour, Jesus Christ. Amen.

The peace

God gives his power to all whom he calls:
he goes with them and gives them his peace.
The peace of the Lord be always with you.
And also with you.

Blessing

God give you the grace to be numbered among his saints,
that you may love him and serve him with joy and in peace:
and the blessing of God Almighty,
the Father, the Son and the Holy Spirit,
be upon you and remain with you always.
Amen.

DECEMBER

St Stephen

St Stephen was among the first seven deacons of the Church and the first known martyr. All that we know about Stephen is in the Acts of the Apostles (6–7). As a deacon he was appointed to look after the distribution of alms to the faithful poor, especially to the widows. It is clear from the speech he made that he was learned in the Scriptures, and what he said was full of eloquence and power. Stephen was stoned to death on a charge of blasphemy by the Jews. While they were hurling rocks at him, Stephen had a vision of Christ at the right hand of God. He died about the year 35. Those responsible for his death laid their outer garments at the feet of Saul who was to become Paul. From early times Stephen became the patron saint of deacons. In the later Middle Ages he was invoked by those with headaches.

Readings

2 Chronicles 24:20-22
Psalm 119:161-168
Acts 7:51-60
Matthew 10:17-22

or

Acts 7:51-60
Psalm 119:161-168
Galatians 2:16b-20
Matthew 10:17-22

Opening prayer

Stephen gave his life in your service.
Good and gracious God,
grant that we may also live to your glory.

Stephen cared for the needy and those needing protection.
Good and gracious God,
grant that we may also live to your glory.

Stephen proclaimed the gospel by his way of living.
Good and gracious God,
grant that we may also live to your glory.

Stephen was filled with the Holy Spirit.
Good and gracious God,
grant that we may also live to your glory.

Stephen had a vision of your glory.
Good and gracious God,
grant that we may also live to your glory.

Stephen sought forgiveness for his persecutors.
Good and gracious God,
grant that we may also live to your glory.

Stephen gave his life witnessing to your love.
Good and gracious God,
grant that we may also live to your glory.

Intercessions

Gracious God, we give thanks for the life and witness of St Stephen.
We ask your blessing upon all who risk their lives to tell of you.
We pray for all who quietly serve and give their lives in the service of others.
We remember all who are being persecuted for their faith or for standing up for justice and peace, especially [...]
We pray for all whose lives are endangered for being Christians.
Lord of life and love:
give us strength that we may serve you.

Gracious God, we give thanks for all who speak up for the poor and rejected: we ask your blessing upon them.
God, give courage to all who refuse to accept discrimination and inhumanity at any level.

We pray for all who stand up against the destruction and degradation of the earth, and the destroying of species.
We remember all who work in rescue work or in conservation, all who care for the planet.
Lord of life and love:
give us strength that we may serve you.

Gracious God, we give thanks for all who serve us in our community.
We ask your blessing upon the social and medical services, the fire brigade and the police.
We pray for all who provide us with water and food, the farmers, fishermen and processors of food.
We remember our local shops, post office, clubs, community and sports centres.
We give thanks for and ask your blessing upon our families and loved ones.
Lord of life and love:
give us strength that we may serve you.

Gracious God, we give you thanks for all you have given us and for our well-being.
We pray for all who are poor and for those in difficult circumstances.
We remember all who are hungry, ill-housed or homeless.
We pray for all who are ill, remembering especially […]
We ask your blessing upon all who are terminally ill, and those in a hospice.
Lord of life and love:
give us strength that we may serve you.

Gracious God, we remember before you St Stephen and all holy martyrs, all who have died giving their lives for others.
We pray for our loved ones departed, that they may rejoice with them in the light and love of your presence. We pray today especially for […]
Merciful Father,
accept these prayers for the sake of your Son, our Saviour, Jesus Christ. Amen.

The peace

Do not be afraid, for the God of glory is always with you and his presence is peace.
The peace of the Lord be always with you.
And also with you.

Blessing

The presence of the Father Almighty,
the peace of Christ his Son,
the power of the Holy Spirit,
and the blessing of God Almighty,
the Father, the Son and the Holy Spirit,
be upon you and remain with you always.
Amen.

St John

Today we celebrate St John the Apostle and John the Evangelist. Whether this is one person or two, we cannot be certain. John and James were the sons of Zebedee whom Jesus called to be disciples (Mark 1:20). With his brother and St Peter, John was privileged to experience the Transfiguration of Jesus, the raising of Jairus' daughter, and the Agony in the Garden. In the Acts of the Apostles John always appears as a companion of Peter and is never recorded as speaking (Acts 3:1; 4:1-13; 8:14) In Paul's letter to the Galatians, John is named as one of the pillars of the Church with Peter and James (Galatians 2:9). The fourth Gospel bearing his name never mentions John but speaks of 'the disciple whom Jesus loved' (John 13:23-25; 19:25-27; 20:2; 21:20). There is also mention of a 'witness' to events (19:35; 21:24). In both these descriptions it is generally believed that it is John the Apostle who is also the Evangelist. After the martyrdom of his brother James, it seems John moved to Ephesus. Tradition has it that it is from there the aged John penned his Gospel. The symbol in art for St John is an eagle, for John presents a visionary image of Jesus, one of his divine nature and of his ascension.

Readings

Exodus 33:7-11a
Psalm 117
1 John 1
John 21:19b-25

Opening prayer

In the beginning, God.
Lord, you are with us always:
may we abide in you as you are in us.

In the beginning of creation, God.
Lord, you are with us always:
may we abide in you as you are in us.

In the beginning of time, God.
Lord, you are with us always:
may we abide in you as you are in us.

In the beginning of life, God.
Lord, you are with us always:
may we abide in you as you are in us.

In the beginning of this day, God.
Lord, you are with us always:
may we abide in you as you are in us.

Intercessions

God of Glory, ever present, we give you thanks for St John the
Evangelist and for the Good News as proclaimed by him.
We ask your blessing upon all churches, places and people dedicated
in the name of St John.
May your Church be aware of the glory of our Saviour, and may we
show that glory in our lives.
Bless all who, though they have not seen you, still believe in you.
We pray for all who by their preaching of the word or through their
lives reveal to us your glory.
Lord, open our eyes to your presence:
and our hearts to your love.

God of Glory, ever present, we give you thanks for men and women of
vision: those who look beyond what is to what could be.
We pray for research workers and scientists, for all who work in
conservation and protection of the planet's resources.
We ask your blessing upon all politicians, and those who decide upon
the well-being of peoples.
We pray for musicians, artists, writers, craftspeople and all who add
beauty to our world.
Lord, open our eyes to your presence:
and our hearts to your love.

God of Glory, ever present, we thank you for all who through vision strengthen the bonds of families and communities.
We ask your blessing upon our homes, our families and friends.
Help us to see where love and care can make a difference to those about us.
We pray for our local councils and organisations and all who help us to live in unity and peace.
Lord, open our eyes to your presence:
and our hearts to your love.

God of Glory, ever present, we give thanks for all who work in medical research and in finding cures for illness.
We pray for our own doctors and nurses, the hospitals and all who work in caring for others.
We remember all who suffer from poverty or bad housing, from war or acts of violence.
We ask your blessing upon friends and loved ones who are ill. We pray especially for [...]
Lord, open our eyes to your presence:
and our hearts to your love.

God of Glory, ever present, we give thanks for all who help us to see that life is eternal.
We pray for our loved ones departed, that they may rejoice in the vision of your glory and rest in your love.
We remember especially today [...]
Merciful Father,
accept these prayers for the sake of your Son, our Saviour, Jesus Christ. Amen.

The peace

The Lord of Glory fill you with all joy and peace in believing,
so that you may abound in hope.
The peace of the Lord be always with you.
And also with you.

Blessing

God in his grace and goodness, grant you an awareness
of his abiding presence,
of his love for all creation,
and his gift of eternal life:
and the blessing of God Almighty,
the Father, the Son and the Holy Spirit,
be upon you and remain with you always.
Amen.

Holy Innocents

The Magi sought information of Herod the Great concerning where the 'king' would be born. Herod decided that he did not want any claimants to the throne and he gave orders that all children of two and under living in Bethlehem should be put to death (Matthew 2:1-18). There have been various attempts to discover how many children died but it was not a large number – possibly anywhere between six and twenty. Because they died instead of Christ, it was considered they gave their lives for him, and so were counted as martyrs.

Readings

Jeremiah 31:15-17
Psalm 124
1 Corinthians 1:26-29
Matthew 2:13-18

Opening prayer

Lord, we still hear of innocents massacred:
Lord of love,
may the world be delivered from such evil.

Villages are being raided and homes destroyed:
Lord of love,
may the world be delivered from such evil.

Family life is being eroded or destroyed:
Lord of love,
may the world be delivered from such evil.

We hear of the sorrowing of mothers:
Lord of love,
may the world be delivered from such evil.

Loved ones are being separated from each other:
Lord of love,
may the world be delivered from such evil.

Intercessions

Lord of love, you came to save a world that often seems bent on its own destruction.
We ask your blessing upon the Church as it makes a stand against evil practices.
We pray for all Christians who speak out for the poor and the oppressed.
We remember churches in areas of opposition and where innocents suffer.
We pray that we may help to bring peace and unity to our own communities.
Father, hear us:
in the name of Jesus Christ, our Lord.

Lord of love, we pray for all who are caught up in war or violence.
We remember refugees and all displaced peoples.
We pray for all who have lost their home and been separated from their loved ones.
We ask your blessing upon all who work for the protection and rights of children.
We pray for The Children's Society in its care for young people.
Father, hear us:
in the name of Jesus Christ, our Lord.

Lord of love, we thank you for our homes and families, and ask your blessing upon all our loved ones.
We remember all who live alone within our communities and pray we may be good neighbours.
We pray for play-schools, nurseries, and local schools and all who have the care of them.
We ask your blessing upon all organisations for young people.
Father, hear us:
in the name of Jesus Christ, our Lord.

Lord of love, we ask your blessing upon Save the Children, and all who work to relieve suffering and fear among the young.

We remember the street children who have nowhere to live and children who are sent out to beg by their parents.

We pray for all children who do not have access to schools or any form of education.

We pray for all ill and suffering children at this time, and remember all children's hospitals.

We pray especially for [...]

Father, hear us:

in the name of Jesus Christ, our Lord.

Lord of love, we remember all families who have lost a child, through illness, accident or violence.

We pray for all who mourn and all who have been bereaved this week.

As we remember the departed, we pray especially for [...]

Merciful Father,

accept these prayers for the sake of your Son, our Saviour, Jesus Christ.
Amen.

The peace

To us a child is born, to us a son is given,
the Lord Jesus who is the Prince of peace:
it is by his wounds we are healed.
The peace of the Lord be always with you.
And also with you.

Blessing

God created you out of love and for his love.
Abide in his love and in his peace:
and the blessing of God Almighty,
the Father, the Son and the Holy Spirit,
be upon you and remain with you always.
Amen.

CORPUS CHRISTI

Corpus Christi

This Festival is kept on the Thursday after Trinity Sunday and is known as Corpus Christi or 'The Day of Thanksgiving for the Institution of Holy Communion'. Christians already mark when Christ instituted the Eucharist, on Maundy Thursday (the day before Good Friday). Because Maundy Thursday is in Holy Week, it was thought necessary to have a separate festival of the Eucharist that would allow the celebration to take place with a greater sense of joy. It celebrates the presence of Christ in the bread and wine and in his people.

Readings

Genesis 14:18-20
Psalm 116:10-19
1 Corinthians 11:23-26
John 6:51-58

Opening prayer

Lord God, you provided the people of Israel with bread in the wilderness.
Lord God, give us today
our daily bread.

Lord God, you provided Elijah with bread by the ravens on the mountain.
Lord God, give us today
our daily bread.

Lord God, you fed Elijah by an angel in the desert.
Lord God, give us today
our daily bread.

Lord Jesus, you fed the hungry with bread by the Sea of Galilee.
Lord God, give us today
our daily bread.

Lord Jesus, you broke the bread at the Last Supper.
Lord God, give us today
our daily bread.

Lord Jesus, you give yourself to us in Communion.
Lord God, give us today
our daily bread.

Intercessions

Lord our God, Father, we rejoice that you are ever with us.
We give thanks for the offering of Jesus on the cross and for the memorial we have in the Eucharist. May we remember that he abides in us and invites us to abide in him.
We pray for all who celebrate the death and passion of our Lord Jesus: for bishops and priests and their congregations. We remember especially [. . .]
We pray for all the newly confirmed and for those who receive the sacraments at home or in hospital.
Bless all who seek to show our common union in you; all who reveal unity and fellowship within the Church and the world.
Lord, as you abide in us:
help us to know we abide in you.

Lord our God, Father, as we give thanks for the bread in this sacrament, we give thanks for the fruits of the earth and for all that you have given us.
As we break the bread, we remember those who are without food and all who are struggling to survive.
We pray for communities and people that are divided, that they may know your reconciliation and peace in their dealings.
We remember lives and spirits that are broken; may they know the risen Lord and his resurrection.
Lord, as you abide in us:
help us to know we abide in you.

Lord our God, Father, we give thanks that Jesus was known in the breaking of the bread at Emmaus.

We give you thanks and praise for our homes, for their peace and protection.

We pray for our loved ones and all who enrich our lives by their goodness.

We ask your blessing upon all homes where there are broken relationships, where there is disunity or discord.

Lord, as you abide in us:

help us to know we abide in you.

Lord our God, Father, as we give thanks for the wine of Communion, we remember the offering of the life of Jesus so that we may have life eternal.

As we give thanks that Jesus has shared in our grief and sorrows, we pray for all who are facing pain or weakness, all who feel diminished by the trials of life.

We pray for all who feel betrayed or deserted and all who are lonely.

We remember those whose energies are failing and any who are finding it hard to cope with life.

Lord, as you abide in us:

help us to know we abide in you.

Lord our God, Father, we celebrate our common union with you and with the whole Church in earth and in heaven.

We rejoice in the resurrection of our Lord. We pray for all our loved ones departed from us: may they with all the saints enjoy the fullness of your presence and your kingdom.

We pray especially today for [. . .]

Merciful Father,

accept these prayers for the sake of your Son, our Saviour, Jesus Christ. Amen.

The peace

We are the body of Christ. In one Spirit we were all baptised into one body.
Endeavour to keep the unity of the Spirit in the bond of peace.
The peace of the Lord be always with you.
And also with you.

Blessing

Abide in the Father and in his light,
abide in the Son and in his love,
abide in the Spirit and in his power:
and the blessing of God Almighty,
the Father, the Son and the Holy Spirit,
be upon you and remain with you always.
Amen.

HARVEST

Harvest

There was a time when the annual harvest was a time of celebration and joy. Now that we get our produce from all around the world and the majority hardly know where their food is from, harvest celebrations have waned. Yet in a time when we seem to be destroying much of the biodiversity of the world and impairing our ecosystem, Harvest Festivals could become a way of celebrating the joy of creation and the need for respect for all creatures, including protecting their environment as well as our own: celebrating that the earth is the Lord's and all that is in it.

Readings

Year A
Deuteronomy 8:7-18 *or* Deuteronomy 28:1-14
Psalm 65
2 Corinthians 9:6-15
Luke 12:16-30 *or* Luke 17:11-19

Year B
Joel 2:21-27
Psalm 126
1 Timothy 2:1-7 *or* 1 Timothy 6:6-10
Matthew 6:25-33

Year C
Deuteronomy 26:1-11
Psalm 100
Philippians 4:4-9 *or* Revelation 14:14-18
John 6:25-35

Opening prayer

For the gift of creation:
God of love,
we give you thanks and praise.

For the intricate web of life:
God of love,
we give you thanks and praise.

For the beauty of the earth:
God of love,
we give you thanks and praise.

For the sun, soil and rain:
God of love,
we give you thanks and praise.

For the sowing and the reaping:
God of love,
we give you thanks and praise.

For the bounty of the harvest:
God of love,
we give you thanks and praise.

For the milling and the bread-making:
God of love,
we give you thanks and praise.

For all you have given to us:
God of love,
we give you thanks and praise.

Intercessions

God, Creator of all, we thank you for the harvest of this year.
As a Church, may we show that humanity alone cannot adequately reflect you: the whole diversity of the earth is needed to give us even a glimpse of your goodness and glory.
May the Church guide us to live in such a way that the marvellous diversity of our planet is respected and preserved.
May we live in reverence for your creation and in harmony with one another.

Lord, teach us to help people to love the world with the great love that you have for it.
O God, our Creator:
help us to love and respect all your creation.

God, Creator of all, we remember all the hard work of those who produce our food: the farmers and fishermen.
We pray for shopkeepers, for those who process, transport and deliver our food.
We ask your blessing upon all who do not earn a fair day's pay for their work.
We remember all those who do not have enough for a proper meal each day.
We pray for all relief agencies and all who strive to free people from hunger.
Help us to share the harvests of the world more fairly, so everyone can be fed and there will be no more starvation.
O God, our Creator:
help us to love and respect all your creation.

God, Creator of all, we thank you for the world we see around us: for the flowers, the trees and the animals.
May we in our homes teach our children not to take it all for granted, but to treat it with love and care and respect.
We ask your blessing upon our homes and our communities, that we may appreciate what we have been given.
We remember any for whom this has been a lean year or a difficult one.
O God, our Creator:
help us to love and respect all your creation.

God, Creator of all, we pray for areas of our world where nature's balance is being destroyed.
We pray for the indigenous peoples of the rainforests and that their land will not be taken from them.
We remember in sorrow all who are ill through humankind's misuse of the earth and all the creatures that are facing extinction.
We give thanks for the great progress in medicine, and we pray for our local hospitals.

We remember before you loved ones who are ill: we pray especially for
[...]
O God, our Creator:
help us to love and respect all your creation.

God, Creator of all, we thank you for our lives and for all who have
cared for us.
We pray for our loved ones departed, remembering especially today
[...]
May they rejoice in the gift of life eternal in your glory.
Merciful Father,
accept these prayers for the sake of your Son, our Saviour, Jesus Christ.
Amen.

The peace

Great is God's steadfast love towards us:
his faithfulness endures forever.
He offers us his peace.
The peace of the Lord be always with you.
And also with you.

Blessing

God, who created every atom,
God who set the sun, moon and stars in space,
God who loves all of his creation,
is the God who is with you:
and the blessing of God Almighty,
the Father, the Son and the Holy Spirit,
be upon you and remain with you always.
Amen.